How to Make Group Psychotherapy Work

Other books written by Dr. Coleman

Life After Crime
Abnormal Psychology
Group Therapy as a Contact Sport
Understanding Counseling and Psychotherapy
Escape the Chambers
Legend of Silver Wolf

How to Make Group Psychotherapy Work

New Perspectives on Group Therapy

Thomas R. Coleman

Print information available on the last page.

Rev. date: 01/14/2026

To order additional copies of this book, contact:
Xlibris
844-714-8691
www.Xlibris.com
Orders@Xlibris.com
720750

CONTENTS

ACKNOWLEDGMENTS

I would like to thank all the clients, students, and alumni who have contributed to the betterment of the ideas presented in this book. Special thanks to Professor Roger Cunningham, who helped write several chapters initially and who has helped run these groups. Professor Cunningham is primarily responsible for the chapter on genograms, and helped create the initial first chapters—"Rationale for Change" and "Healing the Healer."

Also, I would like to thank Reverend Dan Shaw who helped with the development of many of the ideas in the chapter on achievement motivation.

Finally I would like to thank my wife, Jaynie Coleman, who worked tirelessly many hours on rewriting and editing this book.

Why I Wrote This Book: Finding My Way Out of the Darkness

Right after I was born, my mother was sent to a Psychiatric Hospital in Rochester, New York. I think she was there for a few years, and when she came home she complained that she had been dragged kicking and screaming into a shock treatment room where she was knocked into unconsciousness with jolts of electricity. She was told that this would get rid of her depression. The multitude of shock treatments did also have the effect of damaging her memory.

When I remember my childhood I remember it as a living hell. I was sick most the time and my nights were haunted with nightmares from which I would awake screaming and throwing up. I was terrified of going to sleep because an ugly witch would be lurking there. She had sharp fangs and long claws, and she would chase me around Grover Street panting down my back.

Being the youngest of my siblings, and with other giants around me, I was convinced that I was an inferior creature. Common sayings in my house were "Children are to be seen and not heard," and "I will beat the daylights out of you."

Additionally, I had undiagnosed *attention deficit disorder* and *dyslexia*. As a frail and sickly child, I was an easy pick for the bullies at Martin Street Elementary School. When I got home, father would hit me with the boxing gloves to "make a man out of me!" But that didn't work because I simply hid from him and the rest of the hostile world.

Yes, I started life sick, anxious, depressed, and terrified of the world.

Pastor Krentz and Uncle Albert and Aunt Freda Shrader, from my church, told me that God loved me and would protect me, so I decided that I either wanted to be a minister or a psychologist. I chose to be a psychologist so I could find my way out of darkness and despair.

As the years progressed, God and the study of psychology did indeed help me to climb out of the pit. First I found out what worked for me, and made me more spiritually and psychologically healthy. Then I realized I wasn't alone, and I learned what also worked for others to help them out of the pit of despair.

I wouldn't like to repeat the traumas of my life, but I am glad they happened. I came to believe that *if it doesn't kill you, it can make you stronger.*

As a psychologist, I compiled a list of methods and techniques that I noticed really worked to help my clients grow emotionally. Some of the methods (e.g., role playing and primal therapy) I learned from others, but others (therapeutic theater and secrets groups) I developed with input from others. I developed groups using these methods.

As people became interested in attending to these groups, the groups became much larger than the recommended number of eight to twelve people that the graduate courses and training courses suggested. Necessity often had us attempting to develop techniques that would work with not only thirty or sixty, but hundreds of people. We found that there are thousands of hurting people in society crying out for connection, healing, and recovery, but the cost of therapy and finding the right healing modality was too enormous for the average person to fathom.

As a result, Sensitivity Empowerment Workshops (SEW) was established to help larger groups of people. We found that most psychologists, psychiatrists, social workers, and counseling professionals were comfortable with individuals and possibly groups of up to eight to twelve, but were ill equipped to work with large groups of people. In such cases we noticed that "professionals resorting to lecturing" wasn't as helpful or as healing as "experiencing." This book was written to aid the professional in running larger groups in a safe therapeutic manner.

Introduction

WHAT DO YOU DO WHEN YOU RUN A GROUP AND HUNDREDS OF PEOPLE SHOW UP?

Mental health professionals are often more comfortable and trained to run individual and small groups, but need training to treat large groups. This book demonstrates how learning to run larger groups can not only be exciting for all, but also highly therapeutic. In the book are numerous testimonies from individuals who have benefited from Sensitivity Empowerment Workshops and examples of individual growth and healing. Below are accounts of a few clients, with names changed to protect confidentiality, plus the story of HBO's documentary, and subsequent movie, featuring a recovering addict named Deliris.

Tony was a thirty-five-year-old man who struggled through a series of homosexual relationships until he found another more stable relationship with an older man with whom he lived for several years. One day Tony attended our workshop. In a Secrets Group he anonymously presented his *secret*. He said this offered tremendous relief, so he participated in a Sensitivity Group. In that group he confronted his father with the deep-seated feelings he had for him and his indifference to Tony. He then thanked his role-playing mother for being there through extreme poverty. Next he got into deep feeling with several men who had sexually abused him as a child. At the end of the group, Tony asked when the next group was, and he began to regularly attend our smaller therapy groups. Over a couple of years, Tony "experimented" with dating females and found that his search in the homosexual community had much to do with finding a father's love. Tony many years later is happily married and running addiction-recovery groups in his church.

Ron was an African American male whose father was a Muslim and a Black Panther. His parents both used drugs. Both parents were authoritarian, and Ron spent most of his time playing basketball. He was on a college basketball team and an excellent player. Ron was very suspicious of white people and very lustful toward females. He came to my office early one morning and looked very groggy and depressed. He said that he had taken a large bottle of sleeping and other pills because his girlfriend had rejected him and he had given up. He said he woke up after two days very sick to his stomach. He confessed that he was also failing in school and was expecting to be expelled in spite of his stellar basketball performance. I worked with Ron individually, and he attended dozens of my therapy groups and sensitivity groups. He became so charismatic with my clients that I also had him help me lead groups. I also helped him with his academics, and his grades went from failing to As. Today Ron is married with children and an extremely successful social worker.

Matty came to our groups because she was dragged from an NA meeting where she revealed that she was going to kill herself with an overdose of heroin. She had given up. In the group, I noticed that she became hysterical and had to be held and comforted by her friend and one of our SEW workers. At the end of the group session she disappeared, but every large group session after that I saw her, and with her were others she had brought from her NA meetings. I recognized her in the crowd, but she did not come forward. After at least six groups, I was able to talk to her. She gratefully told me that these sensitivity groups had saved her life. With her charismatic energy, she was helpful to our groups. Matty became a minister and has helped hundreds of people herself.

Luke, forty-five years old, came to my group in a drug program and was "skin and bones" from using crack. He couldn't contain any of his feelings and cried copiously in each session. He was frightfully full of shame and guilt and had suffered an incredible amount of abuse in the streets from the method he had used to get money in the streets. He was truly a battered wreck of a man. He was at the bottom. Luke was what we call "sick and tired of being sick and tired." Usually clients have to be told that if they want to get well, they have to be "totally, completely, and brutally honest." Luke didn't need that talk because he wanted so badly to get well that he let it all out. Luke attended all of the sessions that he could, and he learned so much so fast that I would let him take over my group; his testimony and example became so persuasive and compelling. He started to gain weight and confidence and became a counselor in that drug program. He attended college, and when he was available he would show up to a group and electrify the attendees with his testimony and skill. Over the years he earned a master's degree, and he became an assistant director of a large substance-abuse program. He also taught college courses on evenings. People looked at him as an unbelievable miracle. Often in group he would sing, "His eye is on the sparrow and I know he's watching over me." Unfortunately, his years on the street got the better of him, and he died from cancer. Luke was an inspiration to all who knew him.

Starting in 1980, HBO documentarian Jon Alpert filmed a program series called *Life of Crime* following three drug addicts for over 30 years in the streets of Newark NJ. This real-life series, however gory, was streamed on television.

The first two died from consequences of substance abuse. The last person surviving was Deliris Vasquez, an attractive young Puerto Rican mother with three children. Despite efforts, Jon could not entice Deliris to remain drug free.

One day while Jon was preparing to film her in a hotel in downtown Newark, Deliris was cooking a syringe full of "dope." Jon had the sense of not filming the horrific scene, and he left the hotel soon after, depressed and disgusted. He gave up hope for Deliris and left her for dead. He ended the HBO streaming series, too upset to film her demise.

Hours later a sober friend found Deliris, threw her in the shower, dressed, and dragged her two miles down Broad Street to the huge gymnasium at Essex County College. A large group was being run by Dr. Thomas Coleman, Professor Roger Cunningham, and members of the ECC Mental Health Club, Christian Fellowship Club and Bible class. They were gathered to participate in a "sensitivity group."

In that group Deliris sat with a group of twelve other females and for the first time secretly confessed her sexual abuse secrets and criminal activities. That first night Deliris reported that she felt so much relief (see the Bottle Theory of Emotions) that she stopped using drugs and prayed for Jesus to forgive and save her. After that experience she continued to attend both large and small groups and worked on numerous therapeutic issues. Her honesty and motivation encouraged others, and she became a spokesperson for NA groups in the United States, Puerto Rico, and South America.

Four years after the initial sensitivity group where she stopped using drugs, Deliris contacted Jon at HBO and asked him to film her as she received her four-year clean Narcotics Anonymous award. Jon was amazed and astounded to meet the new Deliris. As a result, for the next four years Jon Alpert followed Dr. Coleman to his various groups to record Deliris's electrifying testimony. Deliris rescued and motivated huge numbers of people and Jon recorded many groups with Dr. Coleman. The work that Deliris accomplished was featured in the expanded documentary, *Life of Crime 1984-2020*, and was featured at the Venice Film Festival, New Jersey Film Festival, and the New York Film Festival.

Moving forward, Dr. Coleman was asked to write a companion book, *Life After Crime*. If you benefit from reading *How to Make Group Psychotherapy Work*, please read *Life After Crime*, which chronicles in "memoir format" healing techniques and recovery stories. To contact Dr. Tom Coleman, he can be reached at thomasrcoleman1@gmail.com.

Chapter 1

Rationale for Change

Sitting around a candle, in a darkened room, with five young men, each under twenty-one years of age, in a youth prison return program, the first youth begins:

> I was 14, dealing drugs, we went for a deal. Someone gave me a gun. We went into an apartment, but something went wrong. I pulled my gun. It went off. I opened my eyes, and there were gun casings and blood all over. Three people were dead. I don't know what had happened.

> The next youth says,

> I can identify with that. My little brother and I were playing alone in the apartment. He found a gun and showed it to me. I had never seen a gun before. It went off and killed my brother. I will never see him again.

As we went around the room, I realized I was sitting with five young men who had killed eight people among them. They had been released from a youth prison, but were now in a holding program, until their parents or guardians were located. We put our arms around each other and sobbed as we sang along to "You are not alone. I am here with you."

These are not the stories that a clinician often hears, but this story is real and the theme is the same. Incarcerated people are tough, hostile, unemotional, and often not able to cry because tears are considered weakness, and in prison, the weak are preyed upon.

People not in prison may also be hardened emotionally, and many have difficulty expressing honest feelings and emotions. Clinicians are required to provide services for each type of client. Is the average therapist able to reach this client in a meaningful healing way with the tools received in one's education and training? Experience has shown us that many are not.

Or how about a clinician who is working with a group of unauthentic suburban wives with children who are ready to cast off their families in a quest for a more fulfilling or satisfying scenario?

The wife is part of a two-income family and still has to be mother, chef, charity volunteer, chauffeur, and sometimes wife. This wife may have no life of her own. Even though she has access to psychiatrists, psychotherapists, the cutting edge of self-help, nutrition, gyms, masseuses, and tennis lessons, her life seems to lack meaning. One SEW participant was married to a medical professional, had a child, and after an unfulfilling job at a Wall Street firm, decided to return to school to "find herself." She came extremely distraught to her first workshop, ready to divorce her husband, abandon her child, and just try to make it on her own. She was in her thirties, felt she had married too young, had a child before she wanted, and now felt tied down to a workaholic husband. She was very attractive and believed that she would have no trouble finding another man who would be more receptive to her needs. In the midst of a very teary Secrets Group, another member asked simply, "Whose life are you leading, anyway? Why not take time to explore what you want on a daily basis?" The participant responded with a litany of her responsibilities and the inability to take on one more task. The other member responded, "Is it your life or not?"

The participant replied, "Of course it's my life!" to which the other member said, "Then live it like it is yours!" There was another barrage of tears and the participant said, "Yes, I will take time to do what I want to do in my life."

In a later follow-up with the participant, she began to take a little time for herself every week to explore her desires. While nothing so abrupt occurred as leaving her husband and family, she instead found that as she gave herself permission to do what she wanted, she was better able to do the things necessary for her husband, child, job, school, and life. She has completed not only her two-year degree but also a bachelor's and master's, had another child, and has a prestigious job in the field of her choice.

This book is a how-to for both the emerging and the seasoned clinician. Therapy must be an interactive experience. Psychology is a contact sport with rules, principles, and techniques where everybody (client and therapist) wins. The challenge for the twenty-first-century therapist is to enable both the toughest of tough client and even the not so rough to grow into emotionally healthy individuals who can move forward with productive and healthy relationships with self and others.

Refer out is the panacea for many therapeutic situations. The schools, the courts, and the parents all look for the trained clinician to have the magic wand and to be the fixer to cure society's problem child. Recently psychology was one of the most popular majors offered at the college level. The need for workers is so great that many students begin working without completing their training. What can they be offered to allow them to relate to their clients?

Dr. Coleman and Professor Cunningham have worked thousands of hours of group therapy over the past forty years and were frustrated by many of the techniques learned in graduate school. What looked very fine on paper, when one walked into a room with thirty convicts, each with an average of twenty years in prison hanging around his neck, experience quickly revealed that the traditional nondirective approaches did not work. Therapy sessions became opportunities to complain and to express irritation and hostility and to rationalize behavior, with little effective resolutions and change offered. None of this is very therapeutic.

The realities of working in the field of group counseling often dictate parameters that are out of bounds of the traditional guidelines for running groups. For instance, existing counseling books suggest there should be no more than twelve participants in a group; however, the realities of rehabilitation programs may mandate otherwise. Today's practitioner can conduct groups from ten to four hundred people. Traditionally trained group therapists melt down in such atmospheres.

Group therapy needs to be interesting and dynamic, as well as effective, for both the leaders and the group members. Clients who are very easily bored can use their manipulative techniques in the group so that the group often ends in a power struggle, rather than being a healing environment. Hundreds of clinicians feel defeated by their clients at the end of some sessions. Dynamics can become so hostile and certain elements become so adversarial that many counselors burn out quickly. Many populations desperately need healing, and yet many counselors are clueless how to work with these populations. Clinicians either bore clients with theory or just lecture for the session they are required to be with the client.

The recidivism rate in our prisons and juvenile halls is abysmal. The recovery rate in our public run drug programs is also awful. The divorce rate and the breakup of the family does not stop. If Ford Motor Company turns out one hundred cars in its assembly line and only twenty of those cars run, how long would Ford Motor Company remain in business? Yet billions of dollars are invested in "correctional institutions," "therapeutic communities," and "mental health facilities" with what kind of recovery rate? Clinicians need to examine carefully what they are doing, why they are doing it, and how to develop new ways to reach clients, especially hard-to-treat clients, in order to improve treatment. We have noticed that too many therapists fall back on traditional and more comfortable treatments, rather than challenge themselves to learn newer, more effective ways of running groups.

Current group therapy practices are in the diaper stage. The professional community should not be satisfied. The old techniques cannot be taught as orthodoxy. Clinicians need radical, new, effective techniques that reach deep into the clients' psyches, heal their broken hearts, and inspire them to develop healthy ways of fulfilling their needs in the real world.

With this mission in mind, Coleman and Cunningham embarked on a journey to reinvent group counseling. We used questionnaires with clients and interviewed clients for suggestions on improving counseling. What worked best and what therapeutic methods should be tossed out? We examined the recovery rate from our groups and found that our group members had a much higher recovery rate than the clients who did not attend our groups. These results inspired and empowered us to write this book.

Our experiences in conducting groups led us to develop a system in group therapy and counseling called Sensitivity Empowerment Workshops. The term *sensitivity* has nothing to do with the traditional sensitivity groups of the past. It simply means that the aim of Sensitivity Empowerment Workshops is to make members more aware (sensitive) of their internal dynamics so they can learn to have more control (empowerment) over themselves and grow mentally, emotionally and spiritually healthier. *Empowerment* refers to helping the group member become more effective and integrated so he or she can live a more fulfilled life. *Workshops* are group sessions designed to help people grow. These workshops are designed for anyone, regardless of an individual's personal background or current circumstances. While much work has been done with difficult populations, quite often counselors refer individual clients to attend the Sensitivity Empowerment Workshops as part of their therapeutic journey.

Underlying principles for Sensitivity Empowerment Workshops include four basics.

1. **Therapists can only take the client as far as they themselves have been**. Every future clinician must work on self first. In order to show clients how to melt their frozen tears, group facilitators must first be able to cry. If a person can't identify with his own pains, his therapeutic approach may be distant and cruel. One must first experience his pain and joy, before he can lead another to her pain and joy. Sensitivity Empowerment Workshops require each group leader to participate in a minimum of three sensitivity groups before he or she is able to facilitate one of the smaller groups.

2. **Therapy should be fun**. No one wants to engage in therapy if it is totally painful or dreadfully boring. Therapy must integrate fun, interesting involvement as a vital part of the process of becoming healed. A healthy person can learn to laugh and be playful.

3. **Therapy is painful**. The clients must face issues that they have previously avoided or run away from in order to be healed. The adage applies, "Weeping lasts for a night, but joy comes in the morning."

4. **Therapy must offer hope.** Without hope, there is no future. For many God is the hope. "I am the Alpha and the Omega." God is an instrument in the healing process. We have found that a client who has hope for the future in a loving God has a much higher chance of recovery.

Sensitivity Empowerment Workshop
Six Hours on the Gymnasium Floor
Reflections on Change

The recorded words of others often best describe an experience. One anonymous participant writes:

With the bustling activity and seeming confusion of setting up a rock concert, a sound system is installed, youth begin to wander in, dressed in all their street finery, carrying pillows, blankets, some even with teddy bears; dance music begins, the youth slowly start dancing, moving around. Some people arrive wearing red T-shirts, collecting candles, 3x5 cards, and pencils. The red T-shirts (trained counselors) start encouraging those standing around to start dancing and soon the room is pulsating with the electric slide or the cha-cha slide. A low-brow disco has been created.

> The music starts pumping and the red T-shirts come to the front of the hall and the leader with the microphone says, "Imagine you are surrounded by canvas and you are a famous painter, and there is a bucket of paint in front of you. Now, dip your hand in the paint and start painting the canvas in front of you, and now the wall to your left and now the wall to your right, behind you, paint the ceiling, now the floor." And in a seemingly rhythmic trance, the entire room is being 'painted' with a rock beat.
>
> "Now dip your foot in and paint the wall with your foot . . . Now dip your head in and paint the floor with your head . . ." And soon everyone and everything is covered with the imaginary paint. Everyone is laughing and good feelings engulf the room. Even the wallflowers and sourpusses have warmed up.
>
> People continue to wander in, looking somewhat confused, shy and not knowing what to do, but the music and the dancing entice them to the dance floor and their presence is hardly noticed. Over the course of the next hour more than 300 students, professors, professionals, residents and counselors from drug programs, homeless shelters, and other facilities arrive.

There is more dancing and the devil gets his due in the *Gospel Slide*, and *Stomp that Devil Down!*

The Sensitivity Empowerment Workshop formally begins with a non-sectarian prayer and introduction of the red T-shirts, who are to be the group leaders. The red T-shirted leaders begin to form groups of about ten people. Everyone in the group should be a stranger. Each group forms in a circle around a candle. The leader passes out 3x5 cards and pencils. Everyone introduces themselves, unaware of who we are on the outside; student, homeless, addict, professional, and it seems as if none of us, except for the leader, has any idea what is going to happen.

We are asked to look at our hands and state, "With these hands I have." Then the leader says, "With these hands, I have hit my wife." And we go around and around, with each participant stating, "With these hands, I have stolen, cheated, hurt, abused, gambled, rolled joints," all those negative things that have held us individually from achieving our goals.

There are, of course, a few rules, like Confidentiality. What is said in the room, stays in the room, No Judging and No Laughing at anyone. Our leader explains about the Secrets Group and we each write our 'worst secret' on the 3x5 cards. The participants look bewildered, but slowly write something. The leader collects the cards, shuffles them and passes them back out. We each read the secret on the card we received. The first secret is "I stole $5 from my mother." The leader looks dismayed. The second secret is "I kissed my sister." The leader collects the cards, tears them up, passes out new cards and says, "Let's get serious. I want your deepest, darkest secrets. No bullshit!"

One the second reading of secrets, we hear "I am confused about my sexuality, I think I am gay." "I killed a man." "I embezzled $10,000 from work." "I can't read, nobody knows." Somehow, these, too, seem unreal.

Murder? $10,000? Not in this group! The leader looks pleased, however.

As each participant is encouraged to put himself behind the card writer's eyes and tell a story about the secret, the feeling that the secret is in fact true becomes evident. No one really admits to his or her secret. But my secret was true, and as it was discussed in the group, I felt a big weight come off my chest. I felt like I could breathe for the first time in my life.

We ended the group, arms around each other, singing, *I Need You to Survive.* My heart was soaring! I said a silent prayer, "Dear Lord, please do not let me feel so oppressed by my own secrets again!"

After a short break, some snacks, and more dancing, we again circle our group around the candle. The leader of the entire event now asks us to scream, scream at the top of our lungs. The noise is deafening! He then asks the leaders to scream, then squeeze the hand of the person on his left and that person scream and squeeze the hand of the person on his left around the circle. Then we all scream three times together. Bloodcurdling screams! My body is trembling all over. I notice many people crying. We put our arms around each other and sing "I want to know what love is by Foreigner.

The leader asks us to lie down on our backs, close our eyes and the leader begins a story about meeting someone who has a package for us. We are to imagine accepting this package, opening it up and finding inside, a beautiful photo album, with our name embossed on it.

I notice for the first time that music has been playing throughout the entire evening. It is more ubiquitous now that we hear the commentator introduce, "Your mother has come to see you and you have many things you need to tell her." A woman role playing mother comes over the microphone and asks, "How do you feel about me? Do you love me? Do you hate me?" The participants are asked to shout out their feelings to mama. All kinds of feelings are yelled back at "mama" as well as sobbing, anger and apologizing for evil things they might have done.

Father is totally different. "I hate you. Get lost. Why did you leave me?" A totally different feeling is expressed. I had both parents, so my feelings don't differentiate that much, but I put my arms around the guy next to me. I can feel his body heaving as he sobs for his father.

As the first chords of *Gangsta Lean* are heard, people are openly weeping. I look outside my group and notice two bodies, a male and a female, role playing deceased persons, covered with sheets, with candles at their head and feet. We are asked to come forward to the bodies and offer our last regards to someone we have lost. I am pretty calm, but the song changes to *Last Song* about a man dying of AIDS. I have on the shirt of a friend of mine who died of AIDS this past spring. While it was not like my Mother or Father, I still wanted to say good-bye to Brian. I knelt and was surprised to find tears welling up in my eyes. I remembered the first person I knew that died of the virus. Although it was someone I hardly knew, I had burst into tears and had to leave work that day.

My leader, asking me to come back to the group, shook me out of my reverie. The two bodies had disappeared and I was led back to the group. We were given a new 3x5 card and asked to write what we wanted to pray for and what we were thankful for. I am not too certain what I wrote, but the cards were collected and I chose a card written by someone else. I certainly know what that person asked for and what that person is thankful for, even though I do not know who wrote the card. I am lying in bed now, looking at this card, and as instructed, I am praying for this person every day, for what he or she wants and for what this person is thankful. I don't know if that person ever received his desires, but I know that seeing that card has moved me to prayer more times than if the card was not hanging there.

The Sensitivity Empowerment Workshop ended with all of us in a big circle, with a final prayer and then all dancing "Stomp." I left the Workshop, with my cheeks still stinging from the tears, feeling maybe for the first time the crispness of the air outside, the smell of the damp pavement, and the sound of the breeze. I felt alive, I felt renewed, and I felt rejuvenated. I don't know if anyone could notice the change, but I certainly felt it!

For the past thirty years of running groups, clients and group participants have identified our techniques and practices as "Sensitivity Groups." Some clients, particularly those that are in mandated rehabilitation programs, have difficulty with the term "psychotherapy." They often equate "psychotherapy" or "counseling" with an insinuation that they are crazy. To create a more benign term, Sensitivity Groups became popular. Even though our groups do not have much resemblance to the traditional sensitivity groups, we stay with the term because of our reputation within the New Jersey area.

The student newspaper at Essex County College, Newark, New Jersey, told the story as early as April 1995. Noelle J. writes:

> From the moment I arrived at the Sensitivity Group, I felt a sense of love and unity. It was a beautiful sight, seeing so many people loving and supporting each other. Not to mention that everyone in the room were practically strangers. There were people of every background, everyone with the story to tell. Though each story was different, it was the same, it was a pain that someone, anyone could relate to and understand. At first I was a little reluctant to participate, but when I saw how much everyone cared, it was very easy to open up. There was more love in that room, than in some households. With the attendance of approximately 300 people, there was a lot of pain, but . . . there was also a lot of healing . . ."

Another participant, Melinda H., reports:

> What happened next lead to emotional bursts throughout the entire assembly. Music and then the voice of Dr. Coleman was heard narrating an imaginative

story that pinched many nerves in the room. It had people in the room screaming things like, 'I love you mom' and 'I hate you dad.' Many vented while others comforted those who were crying.

After all the crying and the symbolic burying of those who have died there was more dancing. After everyone was pumped up from the dancing we were split into many groups that were led by group leaders all wearing red shirts. The mood was changed when candles were lit and the lights were off. In these intimate groups of about ten to twelve people we shared secrets anonymously with index cards. They were mixed up and passed around read and discussed. Those who wanted to tell their story, the others stayed anonymous. The evening ended with a lot of hugging and sad good-byes to people you may never see again. This is an event I will look forward to next time. The only thing I recommend to the organizers of this event is a bigger space.

Students who have attended Sensitivity Groups have recorded their impressions. These Essex County College students write:

Anna O. reports, "The 'Sensitivity Workshop,' as it was referred to, seemed highly attended by a noticeable diversified population. Different ages, ethnic backgrounds, religious orientation and even people from out of state were present."

Lynette J. states, "The sensitivity group is a place that leads humans to let go of pain and hostility and free up torture and hatred that has been stored inside for a long time. In the sensitivity group the one thing that touched me was when one of the leaders was telling the little story about the little child that received the great big present that was sent to her, and we all had to act as if we were the little girl who had received the gift and you visualized that great gift and how you felt when you received it."

Amanda S. says, "This sensitivity group has been the best experience that I have gone through. I was able to learn that I am only human and that it's okay to cry. I was so used to possessing this image of strength that I felt ashamed to cry until that night. And I could not stress again how good it felt to cry; it felt like all of my problems were washed away with my tears and when my tears dried up, it dried up. I would recommend this program to anyone because it really has changed me in a way I believe a psychologist may not have."

Chandra W. says, "During my entire stay in the sensitivity group I observed that I am not the only one that has problems. I could not believe that men could cry . . . Some of them took a very long time to open up but whenever this had happened tears were flowing like a fountain. Every part of this program was touching and caused people to come out of their 'shells.' I would like to run more groups for you Dr. Coleman and please do not forget to include the *With these hands I have* process."

Shantaio H. shares that "While I was there I felt welcomed and loved by complete strangers; and I liked the feeling. Thank you for a memory that will last me a life time."

Diana A. adds, "The Sensitivity Empowerment Workshop has allowed me to set goals and standards. You have inspired me and helped me to understand that "if anyone can make it, I can make it! You may not know, you touched my life, but you did. And I want to say thank you."

Additionally, community leaders and community participants recorded their experiences.

Edward Lyons, LCSW, LLADC, LLS, chief clinical officer and executive vice president at Integrity, Inc., states, "I have seen countless numbers of our clients begin to heal from deep emotional wounds through participation in Dr. Coleman's groups."

Ray T., currently a successful rehabilitation program director, recalls, "I had just been released after 15 years incarcerated. I was determined to make a life for myself in spite of my past . . . Dr. Coleman asked me if I would like to attend a sensitivity group. I had never heard of anything like this and was hesitant to go; but out of curiosity I went and this was my first experience with a sensitivity group, particularly the secrets group. It was in these groups that I finally was able to share my fears. Not only did I benefit from them, I learned how to facilitate them. It is 13 years later, I've learned to express my feelings constructively . . ."

Pastor Gennie Holte, of Ray of Hope Church, Newark, NJ, says, "I have worked with Dr. Coleman for several years in many types of groups. I have witnessed people saved from addictions, anxieties, phobias, depression and other issues. I have even seen many members of my congregation energized and transformed. I have witnessed people come away from his groups with greater faith, hope, and courage."

Robert Williams, director of outpatient for a NJ-based drug rehabilitation program, declares, "There is no more powerful spiritual and emotional transformation one can experience than attending a Sensitivity Empowerment Workshop. God cannot be everywhere so He gave Coleman and Cunningham the gift of healing. What tremendous insights one receives from this experience."

Social worker Murad C. writes, "These groups have helped me in all aspects of my life. I am now a healthier person physically and emotionally because I utilized every group. Now I am able to help others the same way they helped me."

Marvin Haynes, his story found in chapter 15, reported, "As a result of attending this group on a regular basis, I have been able to resolve many deep-seated issues from my past. This group really saved my life. I am alive because of this group and I have seen how this group has helped others too. If you want to learn about the power of groups, READ THIS BOOK."

CHAPTER 2

Teaching the Teacher, Healing the Healer

How can you tell the truth about someone
If you can't tell the truth about yourself?
—Virginia Woolf

As social service agencies send their staff back to school, college campuses experience a change in the age range of students from eighteen to twenty to twenty-eight to forty-plus. These students expect not simply theory, but hands-on clinical work. For numerous reasons, these students have returned to the workforce after perhaps childbearing, being in recovery or incarcerated, divorce, a career change or simply recognizing the need for more education. They are both enlivened and overwhelmed by working, going to school, raising families, maintaining their home, and their personal sanity. Their life experiences are valuable and need to be incorporated as part of their education. This student also offers diversity necessary to be able to handle diverse populations.

A psychology course then becomes not a theory course, but a healing opportunity for the student. The course presents an opportunity not to layer theory onto a student, but to allow the student to accept the theory into his or her sense of being. The primary goal therefore becomes an understanding of self in a real sense of "Who is sitting in my seat?" "Who is this person who showed up today?" What follows are techniques that can begin to allow students to experience who they are.

THE FIRST LESSON: RELAXATION
Don't Take Yourself Too Seriously—
Nobody Else Does

Relaxation techniques are vital tools that mental health professionals use in psychotherapy. Psychologists teach relaxation to reduce fears, phobias, obsessive compulsive disorders, and many other issues that torment and control people.

Physiologists have found that stress greatly disrupts happiness and tranquility in people's lives. Stress causes the energy hormone called adrenalin to surge through the body, triggering what doctors call the fight-or-flight response. Anxiety and worries of the "everyday world" can wear down humans. If this response is turned on too long, it can tear down a person's immune system and also the body's abilities to build cells and maintain the body. Put simply, if the fight-or-flight response is turned on for too long, the building and maintenance functions of the body (i.e., the building and maintaining of new cells or the fighting of diseases or infections) is greatly suppressed and can cause the person to get sick or to have a myriad of psychological issues (e.g., anxiety or psychosomatic illnesses). The flight response is obviously fear, and fear alone can tear down the body by causing insomnia, avoidance, and even mental illness. Hostility is an even more destructive emotion. Hostility taken out on others is certainly very destructive; hostility taken out on self is often called depression, and if severe enough, it could cause a raise in blood pressure, heart attacks, and even strokes, plus self-destructive behaviors where the person tries to hurt oneself. Studies generally conclude that the more hostile a person, the shorter his or her life.

For the first lesson of the first psychology class, turn off the lights, ask the students to put their feet flat on the floor, their hands on their desk, close their eyes, and get in touch with their breathing.

Just relax and focus on your breath. Notice how as you breathe, you begin to relax, and as you relax, you are able to breathe easier and deeper, and as you breathe easier and deeper, you can relax even more. Relaxation counteracts the fight-of-flight response—just like water douses fire. Tension and relaxation are incompatible; if you keep water coming at fire, eventually the fire will be extinguished. Just so, if you keep relaxation

coming at tension, eventually the tension will become
extinguished also. Relaxation is a strong antidote to the
harmful effects of stress.

Let all of your thoughts go and just stay with your
breath. Play with your breath. Notice that your lungs go
all the way down to your belly button and feel the air go
all the way down there and your lungs are all the way
up to your collarbone and feel the air go all the way up
there. Notice that you can breathe into your left lung or
your right lung. And just be with your breath. All your
thoughts and concerns of the day are gone, your worries
about tomorrow are gone and you are simply here with
your breath.

Let the students take some minutes to quiet down and get into the
exercise. Do not answer questions or stop when new people enter. Some
may continue reading or writing. If some remain uninvolved, ask the
class to notice their resistance to participating and what they think that
is about. When the ambience of the classroom is quiet and meditative,
continue the breathing for a couple of minutes and while they are
breathing, explain the next exercise.

In a moment we will begin controlled breathing. Here you will
inhale through your nose to a count of four; gently hold your breath to
a count of 6; and then exhale through pursed lips to a count of nine. So
you will be inhaling four; hold six; exhale nine; inhale four; hold six;
exhale nine.

So now take a deep exhalation, letting all the air out of your body,
take a comfortable inhalation, a deep exhalation, letting all the air out
of your body; and inhale through your nose, two, three, four. Gently
hold your breath, two, three, four, five, six. Exhale through pursed
lips, two, three, four, five, six, seven, eight, nine. And inhale through
your nose, two, three, four; and repeat this for at least ten repetitions,
ending with exhale through your nose, two, three, four, five, six, seven,
eight, nine. And take a comfortable inhalation, a deep exhalation, and
a comfortable inhalation and return to normal breathing.

Now, while in this relaxed state, without opening your eyes, just do a
quick scan of your body, make sure you are comfortable, wiggle around

in your seat or stretch a bit from your seat, and just bring yourself to quiet consciousness.

Bring your attention to your feet. Now, I want you to tense up your feet, roll your toes up and clinch your feet, your feet are tense, your feet are tense, your feet are tense. And while holding your feet tense, bring your attention to your ankles, your ankles are tense, your ankles are tense, your ankles are tense. And while holding your feet and ankles tense, tense your calves, your calves are tense, your calves are tense, your calves are tense; your knees are tense, your knees are tense, your knees are tense; your thighs are tense, your thighs are tense, your thighs are tense; and while holding your feet, ankles, calves, knees, and thighs tense, clinch your buttocks. Your buttocks are clinched, your buttocks are clinched, your buttocks are clinched. Your large and your small intestines are tense, your large and your small intestines are tense, your large and your small intestines are tense; your stomach and your liver are tense, your stomach and your liver are tense, your stomach and your liver are tense. Your heart and your lungs are tense, your heart and your lungs are tense, your heart and your lungs are tense.

> Now, holding everything tense, bring your attention
> to your hands, clinch your fists, your fists are clinched,
> your fists are clinched, your fists are clinched. (This is
> an opportunity to see if the students are participating.)
> Now, bring your shoulders up to your ears, your shoulders
> are tense, your shoulders are tense, your shoulders are
> tense. Your neck is tense, your neck is tense, your neck
> is tense. Your hair is tense, your hair is tense, your hair
> is tense. Now scrunch up your face; your face is tense,
> your face is tense, your face is tense.

Now, your entire body is tense, make your entire body tenser than it has ever been before, tense, tense, tense. And, now while holding your body tenser than it has ever been before, just imagine that you are in a nice summer rain, or a waterfall, or even in your shower. And feel the water fall gently on your hair; your hair is relaxed, your hair is relaxed, your hair is relaxed; your face is relaxed, your face is relaxed, your face is relaxed; your neck is relaxed, your neck is relaxed, your neck is relaxed; your shoulders are relaxed, your shoulders are relaxed, your shoulders are relaxed; the water runs down your back, your back is relaxed, your back is relaxed, your back is relaxed. Your hands are relaxed, your hands are relaxed, your hands are relaxed; your heart and lungs are relaxed, your heart and lungs are relaxed, your heart and your lungs are relaxed. And take a deep breath. Your stomach and your liver are relaxed, your stomach and your liver are relaxed, your stomach and liver are relaxed. Your large and small intestines are relaxed, your large and small intestines are relaxed, your large and small intestines are relaxed. Your buttocks are relaxed, your buttocks are relaxed, your buttocks are relaxed; your thighs are relaxed, your thighs are relaxed, your thighs are relaxed; your knees are relaxed, your knees are relaxed, your knees are relaxed. Your ankles are relaxed, your ankles are relaxed, your ankles are relaxed. Now, imagine you are standing in a pool of warm water and just feel all the tension in your body flow out of your feet into the pool. Your feet are relaxed, your feet are relaxed, your feet are relaxed.

Your entire body is more relaxed than it has ever been in your life. Relish in this relaxed state, wiggle in your seat if you need to, and just scan your body and see if you are holding on to any tension, any troubles and any concerns and let them just flow away. And again, scan your body from the tip of your head to your toes and let any tension just flow away. Let any tension, any worry, any concern just flow away. Just be here with your breath. Just be here with your breath, comfortably inhaling and exhaling. Letting all of your cares and concerns flow away. If there is any tension remaining in your body, breathe into that tension and let it go. Those pains in your back, your knee or stomach, just breathe into it and let that tension go. Just breathe into that tension and let it go. If it doesn't go, ask it what it wants. What does that pain in your back want? Just ask it, "What do you want? What do you need?" See what comes up for you. What can you learn from your body? What can your body learn from you?

See, this begs the question, "Who showed up to sit in your seat today?" "Who is this person?" "How would you define them?" "Who would show up for this class, knowing all the concerns that one has, why did they choose this class?" "While we are interested in Freud, Jung, Piaget, Erickson, we are most interested in you! The purpose of this lesson is to define 'Who Am I?'"

Psychology courses are some of the most popular courses in colleges today. Students and the general public read a myriad of self-help books to find out more about themselves and why they think and feel the way they do. Perhaps the main reasons a person takes a Psych101course is to understand self and others better, and to learn more effective ways of living with self and others. Let's examine the person that showed up in your seat today.

The students then sit in a circle or horseshoe shape, so that we can all see each other and it breaks down that barrier between student and teacher, with no big desk protecting the teacher. When they individually are ready to speak, students introduce themselves. Right from the beginning, the class participants begin to sense, as Goffman says, "what role they want to play." "Let me get it over with. I want to go last. Maybe he will forget me. I don't want to be the first one to go." The healing begins right in the first lesson.

We are all clients.
—Carl Rogers

The class is then questioned, "Did anyone die during this exercise?" It is pointed out that so far, no one has. According to stress studies after death of a loved one, or loss of a job, the next most stressful activity is saying your name in public. Since all the class has done this, they have completed a difficult part of the course. It is all easy now. A humorous sidelight to this method is that often the student that is most hesitant to speak, the one that requires some cajoling to say her name, becomes the one that once that barrier is broken, leads the group to ask, "Why did we ever want this person to talk?"

THE SECOND LESSON: FOCUSING
The First Step to Wisdom Is Silence;
The Second Is Listening.
—Anonymous

Quietness and focusing on the present (mindfulness) helps reduce the fight-or-flight response and aids in helping the person gain life giving relaxation, getting blood pressure and anxiety to lower levels. We now step into the focusing mode, which is vital to learning listening (we usually talk too much) and communication skills, both necessary for a clinician. Let's begin:

Lights off, feet on floor, eyes closed, focus on breathing. Class begins again with meditation and relaxation to quiet the student from the outside world. Mother Theresa stated, *"All prayer begins in quiet."* This is the quiet she is speaking of, the quietness of mind. Letting all the concerns of the day go and just be at one with God.

And as we sit here, eyes closed and considering who is sitting in my seat today, prepare for our next exercise. The next exercise will be done in total silence. You will not speak. When we come back into the room, look around the room and find someone that you do not know and silently agree to pair up. Then without making noise, bring your chairs together so that you are sitting knee to knee with a partner. That means you are not going to talk or drag your chairs across the floor.

Now, exhale deeply, take a comfortable inhalation, exhale deeply, and notice the floor under your feet, the hardness of your chair, exhale deeply. Take a comfortable inhalation, exhale deeply, listen for sounds in the hallway, lights coming in the window, and exhale deeply. Take a comfortable inhalation, exhale deeply, and as you are ready come back into the room, into waking consciousness. No talking, just simply come back into the room.

Now, just look at your partner. Study your partner. Who is your partner? What do you know about him/her? What can you tell by just looking at him/her? Imagine you are in an art appreciation class and studying this work of art, your partner. Notice the highlights and the shadows, the different colorings. No one is all one color. Notice the brushstrokes that the great artist used in creating this work of art. What is the essence of your partner? If your partner was a car, what car would he be, what animal, what flower, what color, what fragrance? Look in your partner's eyes. Will she let you in? Will you let her in? How far can you go into her eyes? Notice what comes up for you as you look into her eyes. What is the resistance that comes up for you? What fears do you have about letting someone in? What fears does your partner have about letting you in?

Now, you have been with a person for five minutes. What does that feel like? Acknowledge your partner, give a hug, if you like. Now, who would like to express this experience of being with another person?

Here you want to spend about ten minutes collecting comments. This is a very challenging and threatening process; several cultures do not allow looking into one's eyes, or permit staring at someone. Others feel it is very impolite. That is all okay. Just notice the comments. You may have a woman being paired with a man or two men being paired together feeling uncomfortable. For example, one participant, noticing how he experienced his partner, questioned, 'Should I be having these feelings about another man?' Well, of course. How you can sit with anyone and not have feelings becomes the lesson experienced.

Now, again without talking or making noise, move your chairs, and look around the room and find someone you don't know and without talking, pair up and place your chairs together so that you are sitting knee to knee. When this is accomplished, have students choose who will be A and who will be B. If there are an odd number of students, the instructor will pair with a student. Now, the A partner will play the role of the Healer. You can be a psychiatrist, psychologist, drug counselor, school teacher, Sunday school teacher, or paraprofessional. You don't have to have letters after your name to be a healer. Decide which role you would like to play, and your job throughout this exercise is to remain absolutely silent. Listen attentively, but say nothing. Respect confidentiality. "What is said in the room stays in the room." Whatever your partner chooses to share with you, you do not repeat. Do not tell his or her story. This is an absolute for the entirety of this course.

> Now, B partner, take an issue in your life that is troubling you and explain it to your Healer. A partner says nothing, B partner starts talking. Again, a minimum of five minutes is given for B partner to discuss the issue. A longer time period may be offered, but for the first lesson, five minutes is long enough. As in traditional therapy, some clients may not talk. This is permissible too. Okay, you have been talking about your issue for five minutes. How does that feel?

Allow about ten minutes for the partners to discuss what happened. Again, remind them about confidentiality and not to tell their partner's story. Listen for comments such as "I never had anyone listen to me before" or "It was so great not to be interrupted." After a partner speaks, ask the Healer for feedback.

All the Healers need to stand and let's give them a
big hand. I want the Healers to walk around the room
and find a new partner. And this time we will exchange
roles. The Healer now becomes the client, and the client
becomes the Healer. Again, the Healer says nothing and
the client takes an issue in her life and talks about it.
Remember confidentiality.

So you have again been sharing for about five minutes. How does
this feel? Notice how much more active the room is. Who would like to
share your experiences? Remember confidentiality. This sharing will
probably be much richer in content. Listen for the Healers to say things
like, "I felt honored to hear her story," "I thought that he was telling my
story." This discussion can go on a bit longer than the first.

THE THIRD LESSON: IMAGERY
Relax Deeply and See What Issues Arise

Lights out, feet on floor, hands on desk, eyes closed, just focus
on your breathing. Notice the quality of the air as you inhale and the
quality of the air as you exhale. Play with your breath. How much can
you inhale? How much can you exhale? How long can you hold your
breath? After inhaling? After exhaling? Be aware that your lungs are
not like balloons, but rather tissue, folded over tissue. The lungs are
so large that if this tissue could be spread out, it would cover a football
field. And blood vessels run through the tissue and oxygen from the air
crosses the membrane into the bloodstream and flows directly to the
heart to nurture the heart and to the brain, to nourish the brain and
then throughout your body bringing nourishment throughout your
body, destroying disease organisms and removing waste products. All
of this accomplished through the simple process of breathing. Just stay
there with your breathing, letting all of your thoughts, worries and
concerns go. When a thought comes up, just notice it and let it go and
bring your concentration back to that point between your eyes, what we
call the third eye, and focus on your breath. And when another thought
comes up, notice it, and let it go. And when the next thought comes up,
notice it and let it go. Then return to the controlled breathing exercise
of the first lesson.

Go back now to the earliest memory you have of yourself, (pause) that earliest memory of the first house or apartment you lived in. And see yourself now, on that street, that first street that you can remember walking toward that first house that you can remember. As you get closer, you notice the door opening and a little child coming out of the house. The child looks very familiar, notice how it is dressed, as you look closer, you see that the little child is you, you when you were a little child. (pause) Approach the child. Tell him who you are, that you are all grown up. Let him know that you know his pain and suffering, and that everything is going to be all right. (pause) Let the child know of all the wonderful friends that are in the future, all the exciting good times and that the child will be a part of it all. Comfort the child. You know what the child's needs are. Tell the child all the things that you wish you had been told. "I love you, I am proud of you, I am so happy that you are a little girl or little boy. You are so brave." (Pause.) Whisper these statements over and over again until you are sure the little child hears them and understands them. Then hug your little child, promise your little child that you are going to come back and visit. Make sure that you do; you now know the way. Watch the little child go back to the doorway as you begin walking away. Notice the little child getting smaller and smaller, then the child closes the door and you walk on down the street. Back down the street.

And take a deep exhalation and a comfortable inhalation, a deep exhalation, a comfortable inhalation and begin to notice the floor under your feet, the hardness of your chair, and take a deep exhalation and a comfortable inhalation, a deep exhalation, and notice the sounds in the hallway and the light coming through the windows or doors, and slowly, at your own rate, begin to come back into the room. Don't get up or move too rapidly; you might be a bit dizzy. Turn on the lights and take time to acknowledge your inner child.

CHAPTER 3

Bottle Theory of Emotions

The more you hate someone, the more you become
like the person you hate.
—Sensitivity Empowerment Workshops

Just as a therapist needs to be aware of his or her own inner child, one must also understand the importance of love and affection as it relates to healthy child raising. When a child is young, a parent needs to develop a heart to heart connection with his or her child. When the parent succeeds in nurturing this bond, the child will cherish it and tend to work hard to maintain this connection. If one parental value is to instill hard work and to achieve good grades in school, the child can be nurtured to be diligent in school because he or she wants to please you. As the child grows older, he will internalize these values and therefore learn to care about himself, thus wanting to work hard and to get good grades. He develops his own sense of self-satisfaction for achievement.

While explaining the positive reinforcement aspects to child raising, at the end of the class time, one student stormed to the front of the class angrily. She stared directly into my eyes and said, "I am a single mother and I am under a lot of pressure at work. I not only attend college, I also have an eight-year-old son named George. He gets excellent grades in school and keeps our apartment clean. I have very strict rules for him and I don't hesitate to use the belt on his butt if he misbehaves. I want you to know I strenuously disagree with your namby-pamby approach to child raising."

"Sharon, I agree with you about enforcing rules in child raising, but . . ."

"Dr. Coleman," she interrupted forcefully, "you are wrong. George is a well-behaved child and I intend to keep him that way."

About six months later, Sharon anxiously approached me with "Dr. Coleman, as you know I am a very hardworking single mother and I demand a lot from my now-nine-year-old son George. Well, last Saturday night I came to my apartment exhausted from a hard week of work and my apartment was a pigsty. Clothes were strewn everywhere, dishes were in the sink, and the bathroom a mess. I yelled at George and told him to clean it up quickly, or I would give him the hide tanning of his life. Normally he would have jumped to it and started cleaning, but this time he just continued to lie on the couch watching the television. I yelled louder and told him I would knock the daylights out of him if he didn't get up and clean up this mess. He just looked at me with a blank expression on his face. So I got the belt and grabbed him by the back of the neck and beat him hard. I was so steamed up. I would have stopped if he would have cried and run to his chores. I would have stopped . . ." Sharon stopped as if reflecting deeply.

So what happened then?" I asked inquisitively.

"I really would have stopped if only . . ."

"Go on, Sharon."

She looked as if in a quandary and said, "As I beat him, he didn't cry or plead as before. It is so weird. He just stood there and took the blows and acted as if it wasn't happening. I even got angrier and I would have stopped if only he would have cried. I must admit I went overboard on the beating and put many bruises on his body. I finally got so exhausted that I threw down the belt and fell on the couch and went to sleep."

She paused. "Something very eerie happened. Normally I would hear his radio playing or hear him walking around the apartment or playing with his toys, but my apartment was deadly quiet. It was strange so I opened one eye to see him quietly standing next to the couch about six feet away from me, just staring at me with his hands at his side. Do you think I have a problem with him?"

"I think you have a serious problem with him."

Several years later Sharon's son, George, dropped out of school and became a drug addict.

Sharon was making a classical mistake that many parents make; she was using "force" or authoritarianism to get the desired behavior from George. This sometimes works when a child is young and dependent but often backfires when he grows and realizes that he has other choices.

(Before the Civil War in America many slaves may have acted like they favored slavery, but few stayed on the plantation after they were freed.)

As Dale Carnegie explains in his classical book *How to Win Friends and Influence People* (1936), if you want to motivate people to do something, you develop a positive relationship with them and encourage them to do the right things for themselves. One cannot *force* someone to have an appetite for something. Sometimes the more intently you want something for your child, the less he or she wants it.

A few years ago a distraught father, Peter, who had been a soccer star in high school and college, came to me and said, "My son, Peter Jr., is in middle school and he is the star of his soccer team. He has won many trophies and championships. He came to me the other day and told me he wanted to play hockey." Peter added ferociously, "He can hardly skate and knows little about hockey. Would you please talk with him and get him back into soccer? He is so good he can probably get a soccer scholarship to college."

When Peter Jr. was interviewed, he explained that the reason he wanted to play hockey was that "My father doesn't know anything about it." Junior described his father's authoritarianism and intensive criticism of his soccer techniques had killed his desire to play soccer.

Peter Sr. was advised to let his son try hockey and just maybe he would find out that it is not for him. The father angrily consented and Junior played hockey in high school but wasn't stellar enough to make a college team. He did, however, love hockey.

The father, Peter Sr. had been trying to live his life through his son, instead of being sensitive to his son's feelings, attitudes, and desires. As Carnegie explains, nurturing positive desires in children works better than force. Just as a parent needs sensitivity to the child's wants, needs, and desires, a clinician must have a basic understanding of emotions and their effects on the person.

Psychology books are filled with various theories: psychoanalytic, behavioral, gestalt, rational-emotive, family systems, and motivational interviewing. All of these theories have significance in contributing to the understanding of group therapy. Sensitivity Empowerment Workshops does not detract from these ideas and theories. Indeed it often becomes further necessary to illustrate the psychology of emotions for students and clients in ways they can easily understand. Sensitivity Empowerment Workshops has combined the concepts from modern psychotherapy with techniques and processes that work to find ways to enable people who traditionally have been very resistant to treatment and to enhance the therapeutic benefit for all group participants is the goal. The bottle theory of emotions is the model developed to translate an understanding of emotions to students and clients alike. Once this concept is grasped, many of the techniques and processes used in a Sensitivity Empowerment Workshop become more meaningful.

Emotional intelligence is the ability to identify your own and other people's emotions accurately, to express your emotions clearly and to regulate emotions in yourself and others (Goleman, 1995: Mayer; and Salove, 1997).   Emotions control what people do, and they often rule people's lives. On the one hand emotions can enhance a person's life, or they can be irrational and ruin a life; likewise a person may not express them and be all consumed and ill from the denial of intense emotions. As we age, our emotions become less positive and joyful. Researchers tell us a child laughs about two hundred times a day, a twenty-year-old about twenty times a day, and most senior citizens almost never laugh.

Imagine the emotional side of a human being as a bottle. What most people would like is for that bottle to be overflowing with love and joy. Why is it then that so many of one's emotions are fears, anger, lust, rejection, and depression? If what one wants are good feelings, why are there so many bad feelings? For example, when a couple gets married, they want all these loving feelings, they believe that it is the beginning of their happiness, and yet over 50 percent of marriages end in divorce and disaster. What happened to all that love and joy that the couple wanted? Why is there so much pain and anger and rejection and isolation that happens in a relationship gone awry?

Figure 1. Bottle Theory of Emotions—Initially

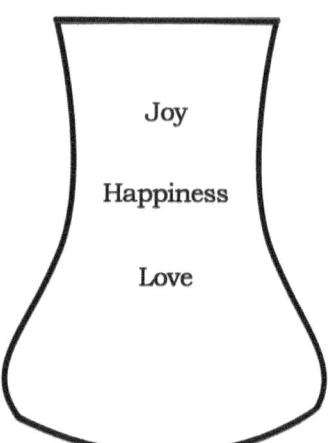

Let's start with infancy and this bottle full of love and joy. What happens to a child who is sensitive and loving and dependent and vulnerable? The child falls down and skins his knee and cries. This is an accident. Or if mother maliciously slaps the child in the face, the child will cry, but in a few minutes will be back in Mommy's lap, saying, "Mommy, I love you. Please don't hit me again." Children are very forgiving; they tend to be very loving, but if Mommy keeps hitting the child, the child learns discouragement and gives up and starts to hide his feelings.

Expression of feeling pain through crying helps children process feelings or emotions and makes them feel better. But if children experience too much pain, they give up and repress and deny the pain. Like George in the example, this pain gives rise to anger and a defensive barrier goes up. If the child is continually abused, the child usually stops crying. Love is pushed down to the bottom of the bottle, joy disappears, and anger turns to hostility. Think of this hostility as a cork on the bottle.

As the child grows older this cork of hostility causes the person to substitute lust for love.

Love is a deep caring about someone, and lust is an uncaring use of an object or a person. A lustful person learns to manipulate and control others. This substitution for love is often the start of addictions (e.g., sex, drugs, smoking, power).

Figure 2. Bottle Theory of Emotions—Learned
Cork (Full of Hostility and Lust)

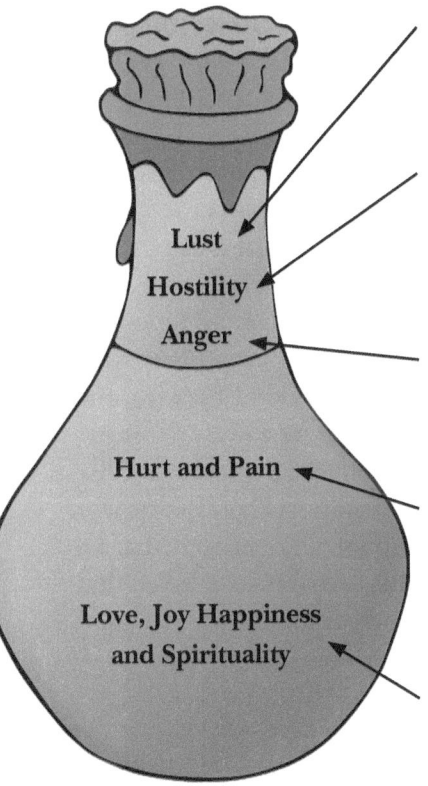

Lust (Replaces love—the person learns to use and to control others. This is usually the start of addictions). This is inside the cork.

Hostility (The person acts superior to feel better about self; can be dangerous. This anger, when turned inward, is called depression). This is also inside the cork.

Anger (Person looks outside self; external locus of control. This is the start of blaming games). Also inside the cork.

Pain and Hurt (What the person is really feeling). These emotions float above the below emotions like oil floats on water. These are the *real issues* to be faced.

Love, Joy, Happiness, and Spirituality (The genuine and good that are buried at the bottom of the emotional bottle).

Figure 2 shows the three basic levels in the bottle theory of emotions. Love is at the bottom of the bottle, pain is filling the bottle, and the cork of lust, hostility, and anger is tightly secured on the top of the bottle. The goal of therapy is to help the client take the cork of hostility off the bottle of emotions; throw the cork away; tip the bottle over and pour out the pain; set the bottle back up; and watch the love and joy and relief start to bubble up and start to overflow. This pouring out of the pain is the healing of the broken heart. A heart heals when it returns to experiencing healthy emotions and to talking honestly about therapeutic issues.

Honesty

"Those whose walk is blameless and who does what is righteous, who speaks the truth from his heart . . . He who does these things will never be shaken" (Psalm 15:2–5).

The emphasis in therapy is on true honesty. "You shall know the truth and the truth will set you free." Honesty is the knife that cuts out the cancer of emotional problems. People who are constantly dishonest, or manipulative, may actually start believing their own lies. Clients who refuse to quit lying often become more hostile, distrustful, and delusional. There are situations when people can get on that slippery slope of dishonesty and slide into the abyss of serious mental illnesses.

When studying the defense mechanisms taught in Psychoanalysis, or the cognitive distortions taught in Cognitive Behavioral Therapy, one realizes how everyone distorts the truth; but the more a person distorts truth, the more one gets out of touch with reality. The delusions (false beliefs) of a psychotic person take it to the extreme, such as the patient on the maximum ward of a psychiatric hospital who believed that he was "god almighty, ruler of the universe." This man was so deluded that he had killed several people who tried to correct him or had laughed at his delusions.

Trust

"Trust is to have faith or confidence in a person or thing because of the qualities one perceives or seems to perceive in him or it . . ." (Author unknown)

Webster identifies trust as "fidelity, consistency, sincerity in action, character and utterance." Trust gives stability to all relationships and is the foundation of interaction with others, as well as with institutions. How many times does one have to lie to a spouse before divorce? How many lies does one tell the boss before being fired? Dishonest people don't trust others because they don't trust themselves. When family members are honest with each other they are more likely to trust each other. Trust goes along with honesty.

Clients constantly hear: "If you want to get better, you must be *totally, completely, and brutally honest.*" The reason why many people are afraid of honesty is because often it is too painful. It takes the cork off the bottle of feelings and reveals the vulnerability of pain, guilt, and shame. But given the right therapeutic environment, this is the honesty that can lead to healing tears and healthy thinking.

The Role of Hostility in Psychological Disorders

While working in jails and drug programs, we have observed that the angrier a person is, the less he cries. Hostile people with broken hearts have much pain but they do not want anyone to see this hurt and pain. On the contrary, they come to believe that honest, transparent people are *weak*. As a result, they go on the attack; they start focusing on others and develop an external locus of control, and play blaming games. This creates a bottle of emotions ready to explode.

One of the first addictions of the addict is anger packed upon anger called hostility. In Narcotics Anonymous literature, a popular saying is that addicts often *shoot dope at their family*, meaning that they blame their family members for the problems they have, thus taking responsibility off the self. When a person is very angry or hostile, he is no longer in touch with love feelings, or natural affections toward others. In a prison, most of the inmates have advanced degrees in hostility. Sometimes a person can't even stare at another inmate without offense being taken. One does not cry in the dayroom of a prison for fear of being ridiculed by other inmates. In prison honest emotion and crying are considered signs of weakness.

In the military, also, emotion is stifled. The sergeant humiliates the private. He literally breaks the private's heart, teaches him to repress his feelings, and instead of experiencing pain, he convinces the private to turn his pain into hostility. Then he gives him a gun and sets him loose on the enemy. A person that is full of hostility feels good when he successfully displaces his own hurt and pain on the "enemy." This symbolic revenge is a kind of emotional *high*. (I.e., if someone constantly humiliates or bullies you, you might be happy to hurt him back or be glad if something bad happens to her.)

Many hostile clients themselves have been physically, psychologically, and sexually abused, but they are in great denial of this hurt. They cover up this pain with anger and lust. They will often swear that their lust feelings are really love. Many men think they are showing love feelings, but are really looking lustfully at a woman as an inferior sexual object. Many men are in denial that this is not love. Moreover, most women who feel like they are being treated like a sexual object, rather than a person, often feel cheated and used. These problems are common issues for men and women.

Lust

Webster defines lust as "to have an intense desire or need." Because the person who is so hostile may no longer experience love, he misinterprets lust feelings as love. Lust has to do with using things and using people as things. Lust feelings come in clusters. A hostile person may develop strong lustful feelings for sex (the most common addiction in males), drugs, revenge, gambling, eating, money, and/or power. Some recent studies have pointed to the finding that hostility jacks up a person's self-esteem artificially. One study found that prisoners in jail have higher (outward) self-esteem than college students. This is a significant finding as antisocial personalities certainly are narcissistic and outwardly do believe they are superior to others.

Clinicians who conduct a group with convicts for the first time often experience rejection and hostility. The clients often act as if they are superior to the therapists. If the clinician took on this image directly and tried to outargue these individuals, he would lose. In most cases this type of client is far more sophisticated, adept, and manipulative in the use of the sword of hostility. Therefore, a clinician should not take on the hostility directly; but try instead to get underneath to the pain and hurt. Help the client look at what broke his heart. Help the client gain the real courage to face his broken heart, to talk and mend that broken heart, so that the hostility can disappear and the person can return to being a loving, joyful person. A real solution to anger management involves teaching the client to take the cork off the bottle and to throw it away.

The Danger of False Pride

"Temper is what gets many of us in trouble. Pride is what keeps us there." This false pride is often an offshoot of hostility. Research studies suggest a humble person often is more psychologically healthy than a hostile person. Experiencing hostility often propels a person to act so superior that he might feel he has the right to hurt somebody else. Also, the person who manipulates another person believes he is better than the other and may try to use the person. "But those who have no pride will be given the earth. And they will be happy and have much more than they need" (Psalm 37:11).

Studies suggest teaching people empty self-esteem can be dangerous. Each person is equally valuable; therefore, it is more important to build a people's self-confidence rather than instill false self-esteem. For example, if someone works for an automotive garage and is the best auto mechanic in that repair shop, does that mean he is a better person than all the other mechanics? No, it just means that he is more capable of rebuilding engines. If this capable person were to generalize his worth as greater than others, and become arrogant and superior acting, he is doing himself a disservice. He may believe he is more superior and more entitled than others. His lack of humility can alienate others. One of the characteristics of a paranoid person is that they are not only hostile but they believe they are superior to others. (They often have delusions of grandeur.) People with these characteristics have extremely poor social skills and invariably ruin their relationships with others and end up as loners.

Research also shows that the more hostile a person, the shorter his life. The more loving a person, the longer his life. Hostility creates stress and drives up blood pressure, makes a person more susceptible to heart disease, causes interpersonal problems, spawns divorce, and generally wrecks a person's life (Sarason et.al. 1999). One day, Dr. Coleman took an informal survey of thirty long-term convicts. Each one had an average of fifteen years of incarceration. He asked them to think of the person in their life who was the most hostile. Then he asked them to surmise where that person was today. Every one of those thirty people agreed that the person they had chosen was dead. The bottom line—hostility kills people.

The Bible states: "Refrain from anger and turn from wrath; do not fret. It leads only to evil" (Psalm 37:8). Also, "Do not make friends with a hot-tempered man, do not associate with one easily angered, or you may learn his ways and get yourself ensnared" (Proverbs 22:24–25).

Forgiveness

"Get rid of all bitterness, rage, and anger, brawling and slander, along with every form of malice. Be kind and compassionate to one another, forgiving each other" (Ephesians 4:31–32).

One very important principle to stress with angry clients is to encourage forgiveness. *The more you hate somebody, the more you tend to become like them.* One client got very angry when he heard that statement. He said his father was a very physically abusive, rejecting alcoholic who abused his mother. Eventually, the man realized that he had become very much like his father with his abuse of drugs, anger at others, and abuse of women.

In the Twelve-Step Rooms, resentment is the first part of the fourth step. "Make a fearless moral inventory." Bill W. of Alcoholics Anonymous states that resentments will cause us to relapse quicker than anything else. The slogan in the room is: *Having a resentment is like taking a poison and waiting for the other person to die.* That is why much time and effort is spent urging clients to forgive. "To forgive is to set the prisoner free and to discover the prisoner was you."

Some studies suggest that men are more reluctant to forgive than women. More men sit in prison, start wars, die in gunfights, have addictions, and are in mental hospitals. Men commit suicide at a higher rate (about four men to each woman). Suicide is often related to depression. Psychologists call depression *"anger in"* because a large element of depression is hostility taken out on the self. Therefore it can be generalized that to a large degree *hostility is mental illness.* From murder, to flying a suicide plane into the Twin Towers, hostility is a great destroyer of society. Our job as therapists is to help clients look behind the hostility, heal the broken hearts, and learn to love again.

"Anger is a mild form of hostility and it can be a friend, not a nice friend, but a friend." (Cameron, 1992). Anger helps us to set our personal boundaries. Anger is an emotion, but many clinicians see it as a secondary emotion (not what the person is really feeling). Underneath all hostility is hurt and pain. We want to welcome our client's emotions, not the acting-out or acting-in of the emotions, but the feeling of the emotions. When a client has been emotionally shut down and medicating his feelings for years, sobriety will begin to free up those feelings. Unfortunately, usually the first emotion to surface is anger.

For many people, anger is culturally the forbidden emotion, so the urge is to medicate that forbidden feeling. Unfortunately, medication cannot selectively isolate feelings, so while drugging anger, the other feelings are medicated as well. One cannot feel elation, love, agape, or happiness while medicated. In order to live a fuller life, one must process the anger. Research verifies that acting out anger only broadens the problem. (Years ago angry clients were encouraged to act out anger by hitting others with encounter bats or by hitting mattresses. The resultant findings were that the more the client was encouraged to do this, the more likely he was to do so in real life.) What needs to happen instead is to identify the perpetrator of the anger, and as difficult as it may seem, *forgive* the perpetrator. Look under the anger and understand the hurt the other person caused and forgive.

One extremely self-destructive, angry addict, toward the end of his treatment, broke into tears as he told of a fishing trip he took with his two nephews. They were in Maine, hip boots in a trout stream, and he found himself crying with the joy of being with his nephews fishing. He realized all the years he had been an addict medicating his anger. He also had been medicating his other feelings and had not appreciated his nephews.

Acting out anger is not the solution—forgiveness is a solution!

Hurt Pocket

When groups are too short to explain the bottle theory of emotion, a shorter explanation of emotions and their effect is the "hurt pocket" image. In his book *The Hurt Pocket*, pastor-counselor Jimmy Evans explains the we all have a pocket in our heart that gets filled with hurt or pain when someone hurts us (physically or emotionally). With time and rejection, that hurt pocket, similar to the pain and fear in the bottle of emotions, will fill up. The hurt pocket can be emptied by sharing the hurt with a trusted friend or therapist, and often is accompanied by copious tears. If, however, the person "stuffs" the feelings in the hurt pocket and refuses to let the feelings out, the pocket can get full and start hurting (e.g., broken heart). If then another person "pokes at the hurt pocket," instead of the response being "you hurt me" (the truth), it will be anger and hostility and the person could lash out (anger and hostility are called secondary emotions). Not learning how to empty the hurt pocket in a healthy manner can lead to all kinds of psychological and interpersonal problems.

Types of Crying

Babies are expressive of feelings while mentally unhealthy people are out of touch with feelings. Babies cry often and often feel relief from their tears when they get their needs met. On the other hand, patients on the most "regressed" wards of mental hospitals generally do not cry, no matter how serious the trauma that they were suffering. Likewise, prisoners in jail, mostly the hardened ones, look at tearful or kind inmates as weak. They usually believe that these people are easy to prey upon. Even in the workplace a demanding boss might perceive a tearful employee as unfit for the pressure of his employment in a highly demanding job. So is crying good or bad? The research has shown that it is either or both.

In high school, the word went out that two young men were mad at each other and were going to have a fight in back of the football field. After school there were about thirty young people in a circle, all male, and the two boys were swinging at each other and trying to avoid the other's punches. All of a sudden the larger boy came around with a roundhouse, and gave the other a bloody nose. The hit boy stepped back stunned and then his face got red and he started to cry. As blood started to pore down his face, his cheeks contorted and an unmistakable face of rage came over him as he dove head long onto the other boy. A vicious brawl ensued. It became clear that the wounded boy was so blindly enraged and ashamed to tears, that if someone had given him a gun or knife at the time, he would have used it. The fight became out of control. The crowd finally broke it up before someone got choked to death or body-slammed on the concrete.

It was at that high school fight that I started to realize that there are many types of crying, and each has different causes and different consequences. Some crying is healthy and some is not.

Stifled Tears

Feelings, a natural part of the human condition, vary all day long. One moment we might be elated, another we might feel disappointed. Today women and children are more accepted than men or boys when they cry. Young males, when a father was spanking him, might hear, "Stop crying." Men have more often denied and repressed pains and hurt feelings because they have been taught from an early age that crying is not being masculine. Men hold feelings in until the bottle is ready to burst.

In the military a person is taught to fight because he is learning to kill people. A lieutenant in the marines bragged one day, "See this platoon. They are the best killers in this man's army!" For males, talking about feelings, and especially confessing fear, is usually taken as a sign of weakness. Above all, letting out feelings by crying is all too often seen as a serious weakness. People in gangs, in jail, and in the military are humiliated, made fun of, and often taken advantage of, if they cry.

Healthy Crying—Crying from Pain and Hurt

Tim, a young man in one therapy group, swore he loved his father and that he was not the source of any of his rage. In a future group the therapist role-played his father and told Tim he was weak, stupid, and that his mother had ruined him. He lost control and screamed savagely at his therapist. After several minutes of cursing at his role playing counselor, Tim started crying, and a child's voice came out of his mouth saying, "I hate you, Daddy, because you never threw a ball with me, you never played with me, you always bullied me and picked on me. You never came to my games. *You never told me you loved me!*"

Tim was weeping from years of verbal and mental abuse and neglect from his father.

At the end of the role-playing session, he looked around the group sheepishly and said, "I'm sorry I made such a fool out of myself." At this, the whole group jumped up and gathered around him to give him a hug. The feedback he got was, "I am so proud of you. It's about time you got real and got those feelings out."

Another male in the same group said, "I wish I could let feelings out like that."

After that session Tim said his anxiety and depression were greatly reduced and he was far more joyful and loving. He even made amends with his father. This client's life began to turn around and his relationships became more loving. He forgave his father, and his father became his friend.

Crying from pain and hurt is extremely therapeutic. It reaches underneath the cork of hostility and lust and gets out the real feelings that have been hidden. Tim finally succeeded in taking the cork of hostility and lust off the bottle of feeling and throwing it away.

Some studies suggest that this type of crying a stress hormone, called cortisol, is secreted from the tear ducts. This chemical hormone is produced by our body to manage stress – psychological, mental or emotional. When a person has a lot of cortisol in his body, he can be extremely nervous and stressed out. Many authorities say that stress is the biggest killer in our society today. This type of healthy crying secretes cortisol to help the person heal from the conditions causing the upset, reduce the stress and bring relaxation.

Clients who loosen the cork of Hostility and Lust and throw it away will get healthier. This however is difficult for most to do because when the cork comes off, the person reveals the feelings he/she has been hiding—feelings like hurt, pain, shame, and guilt. The person goes from "don't feel" to feeling deeply. If he can allow himself to work through the hurt and pain, a more loving person emerges, one who is more sensitive, joyful, transparent, forgiving and resilient. This person is now capable of closer healthier relationships. Likewise, people who are in touch with feelings tends to be physically healthier as well (e.g., lower blood pressure.)

So is hostility a sign of strength? The answer seems to be no. That is why therapists encourage clients to loosen the cork of Hostility and Lust and to throw it away. This is a primary goal of therapy.

Angry Crying—Frustration and Inability to Contain Hurt Feelings

Pete came home from work tired and hungry, and his wife, Flora, was watching television and wiping her teary eyes with a tissue and feeling her body tense. The house was a mess from the children playing in it all day. Tamika, five years old, and Shawn, seven years old, had heard Daddy's key in the front door and ran to their room to hide. Dad often came home from "the grouch factory" in a bad mood, and that was the time of day they most likely got a spanking from him.

"Hi, honey, where's dinner? I don't smell anything cooking in the kitchen."

Flora did not answer. She sat immobile.

"What's the matter?" he asked impatiently. "Tell me what the matter is." He was now shrugging his shoulders and sighing in disbelief.

"Do you know what today is?" she asked.

"Of course I know!" he snapped. "It's Monday and the game starts in an hour. Where's my dinner? I had a rough day today . . ."

"*It's my birthday*," she yelled angrily as she picked up a lamp and threw it at him.

For Flora the cauldron of discontent had been boiling for some time. Each time she cried he ridiculed her and told her to quit acting like a baby. On this day the cork of hostility started to come loose and her real hurt feelings started to show, but to put the cork of hostility back on, she started a big fight. She had given up and she was disgusted with his invalidating comments and insensitive behaviors. She had said to herself, "I am tired of being put down. I am sick of his selfishness. I am tired of him getting drunk every night. I am tired of him mistreating me."

She vowed, "The next time he says something demeaning or abusive, I am going to let him have it! I am not going to let him see what I really feel." What Flora really feels is hurt and invalidation, but she has come to believe these emotions are weaknesses, so she fights back. This hostile stance is dangerous, non productive and unhealthy. The atmosphere becomes toxic when tears are stifled under the cork of rage.

Manipulative Crying—Using Tears for Selfish Purposes

Another type of tearfulness that is dishonest and unhealthy is manipulative crying. This is more often used by women and children. It is a way to get sympathy or to persuade a person to consent to something by giving in and conceding. This behavior usually starts in childhood when a child has a tearful "meltdown" at the grocery store, so that Mommy will give in and change her mind to buy the candy that she previously had told the child she couldn't have. Manipulative crying is insincere and leads to more manipulative behavior and distrust and hostility. It is counterproductive and not therapeutic at all.

CHAPTER 4

What Is Group Therapy?

Love each other deeply, because love covers
a multitude of sins.

—1 Peter 4:8

Group therapy occurs when two or more people come together and show their deepest thoughts, feelings, and memories in an accepting environment so that they grow and heal aspects of their heart (feelings) that are hurting. Therapy is not meant only to heal, but also to learn to love self, others, and God. In the world of psychology, group therapy occurs when one or more trained professionals are on hand to help people resolve therapeutic issues. A therapeutic issue is any problem that the client presents that is seriously interfering with his or her ability to feel emotionally intact and healthy. Usually a therapeutic issue is refusal to accept something (e.g., the death of a loved one) and cope with reality. Not accepting something (e.g., a health issue, a death, a stark reality) is often the first defense mechanism used when a destructive reality faces a person. When dangerous realities face people, they often don't want to face them and thus enter denial (e.g., Didn't Even Know I Always Lied). Denial is a way to soften an intense trauma from consciousness. (e.g., a soldier who lost comrades in a firefight may develop post-traumatic stress disorder—PTSD). Denial reduces a person's ability to cope with reality; therefore, a primary objective of therapy is to help the person learn coping skills to face reality (i.e., acceptance).

People are highly gregarious creatures. They spend much of their day in formal and informal groups. They all have a need to relate and be accepted by others. Group pressure has a very strong pull on an individual. Most addicts will admit that the reason they got drawn into drugs was through group pressure. Often people do things, both good and bad, in groups. Things they would never do alone. Some sociologists suggest that because of the breakdown of the family and society, many people are looking for groups to which they can belong. These groups could be in a church, a bar, a community organization, a pure self-help group, or a family gathering.

In previous centuries, the United States was mainly an agrarian society. In 1870 and before, more than 50 percent of the population worked on farms. The families then were larger and more extended. It was common for grandparents and relatives to live together; women cooked together, had babies together and men helped build each other's houses and barns. Today, less than 3 percent of the people work in agriculture; cities are proliferating. Ironically, much of the community feeling is lost in large cities. With the breakdown of family today, single parents head a large proportion of families. The corporate world has moved from the sense of community found in offices to airport conference centers, cubicles in regional offices, and teleconferencing. Grandparents move to "retirement communities" where grandchildren are banned from staying over extended periods of time. With the onset of modern media and communication options, people are interacting face to face with each other less and less. As a result there is a tremendous resurgence of interest in groups of all kinds (e.g., political groups, self-help groups, therapy groups). When Sensitivity Empowerment Workshops runs a group, open to the public, hundreds of people show up, and most of the people attend through word of mouth. It seems that people crave human contact.

Types of Groups

Therapy and counseling groups are generally under three main categories—prevention, remediation, and self-actualization.

PREVENTATIVE GROUPS

These groups are often education or discussion groups to give facts to help people make wise choices in society. Preventative groups are important because "a stitch in time saves nine." Sensitivity Empowerment

Workshops has discovered that people of all ages have therapeutic issues that need to be worked on. Some participants might say, "I don't need therapy; I am not crazy." However, when you run involved, informative groups that teach individuals how to fulfill their needs and the needs of others in a responsible manner, time, and resources invested as preventative measures saves casualties later. One example is AIDS prevention groups. The value of Prevention Groups is often overlooked, but erroneously so.

REMEDIATION GROUPS

These groups are most likely to be counseling and psychotherapy groups designed to help clients resolve problems and overcome psychological disorders. Remediation can be preventive.

1. *Self-help Groups.* Years ago the main self-help group was Alcoholics Anonymous or AA. Today there are a large variety of these self-help support groups (sometimes called crisis groups) covering a variety of societal problems. There is Narcotics Anonymous for those addicted to narcotics. AA and NA also hold groups for family members. There is Overeaters Anonymous for food addiction, Tough-Love for parents with difficult children, and others for people with cancer, sexual disorders, etc. Self-help groups may not have a professional running them. They are a collection of individuals with similar problems, e.g., people struggling with alcoholism coming together for mutual support and a feeling that they are not alone. These groups are generally free.

    Since self-help groups do not have a "professional" running them, many psychologists and psychiatrists severely criticize these groups. However, Sundberg et.al. (1983, p. 359) says, "Although professionals sometimes look askance at self-help groups because of the quasi-religious nature of same, they deserve our deepest respect. One to one therapies or even therapy groups may have better research and perhaps higher social acceptability, but in terms of the numbers served and the practical, durable nature of the help, self-help groups are a powerful force indeed. In recent years many psychologists have realized their value and have come to understand them, not as competitors in treating people, but as a valuable community resource with unique capabilities." If you want to find out more about self-help groups, want to do a referral, or want to join such a group, the number of the Self-help Clearinghouse is 1-800-formash. Use the Internet to find local self-help resources.

2. *Marathon Groups*. Another remedial approach is the marathon group. Marathon groups are therapy groups that are usually run for twenty-four hours or more. It is believed that when people are tired, their defenses wear down and they are more likely to be honest and open about issues. Many different techniques are used in these groups. The methods used in these groups depend on who is planning and leading the group. One thing that is often done in marathon groups is having each person tell his or her life story from earliest memory to the present.

3. *Psychodramas*. Marino (1946, 1959) developed this type of therapeutic "role-playing" for members of the group to act out one's life, fears, fantasies, etc., as an actor would on a stage. The director of the psychodrama is the therapist and the members role-play a variety of people or auxiliary egos (auxiliary egos are different points of view or aspects in a person's head) as the director suggests. For example, if the client had a difficult relationship with his father, he would have the client choose someone to play his father and he would interact with this role-playing father, saying the things that he would like to tell him. Later the therapist might suggest that the client do a role-reversal, where the client plays his father and the role-playing father plays the client. This gives the person a unique insight into his father's point of view. With the therapist and audience participation, the client can gain insight, catharsis, and self-understanding. SEW uses role-playing and psychodramas to bring the past into the present and to discover hidden intense feelings brought up by role-plays. This can be very therapeutic. SEW has developed a new twist on psychodrama called "Therapeutic Theater." We have found it to be a powerful method of helping an individual with a deep issue. (See chapter 9.)

4. *Group Psychotherapy*. Marino coined the term *group psychotherapy*. In group psychotherapy, members discuss their problems and gain feedback and insight from other members. Group therapy is helpful in encouraging the client to ventilate long-repressed

feelings, gain more effective social skills, and become more effective in society.

The term *psychotherapy group* may be viewed as a stigma to many people and sometimes makes them reluctant to attend such a group. Many psychologists therefore have reframed the groups with names like motivational group, personal issues group, or mental health group. One woman who has had several "nervous breakdowns" is proud to tell people that she attends a weekly "High Performance Group."

SELF-ACTUALIZATION GROUPS

These transformational groups are meant to go beyond psychotherapy and help people find fulfillment and meaning in life. Self-actualization groups tend to focus on the future, can lead to a spiritual awakening, or simply can help the client develop higher vocational goals. These groups are often large group experiences for individuals to come together for a short time, even only one session, to work on improving the quality of life. Marriage enrichment is for married couples to meet in large groups, and also as couples, to help enhance their experiences as a married couple. Other transformational groups are Sensitivity Groups, EST, and Marriage Encounter.

Transformational groups are very cost-effective and can be highly therapeutic if run professionally. Sometimes unqualified people have run groups and can be very damaging. SEW regularly runs groups on topics such as "Coping with stress," "How to thrive in your marriage," or "How to drug-proof your family." One group that is popular for people struggling economically is based on the research of Harvard University professor Dr. David McClelland and is a seminar on being successful educationally, professionally, and economically. Where therapy groups are used to heal the past, the success seminar is used to motivate the person into the future. (See chapter 14.)

Curative Factors of Group Therapy

What does a group offer its members? Yalom (1975) identifies some of the curative factors that a group presents to its members.

1. *Imparting Information.* In a group the members are constantly learning. Group members share knowledge with each other while the group leader also shares information and offers guidance to the participants. This educational component is invaluable because the client gains knowledge about the world and how it works beyond his own individual sphere.

2. *Catharsis.* Catharsis means to get feelings out and is a vital part of therapy. Group members learn how to express feelings in a safe, non-judgmental environment. Expressing the pain of a broken heart, and teaching the person to talk honestly about feelings and crying to get out hurt feelings are all very healing. In the right atmosphere, the expression of feelings builds honesty, trust, relief, and understanding. SEW spends a great amount of time using numerous emotive techniques to encourage emotional relief and anxiety reduction in these groups.

3. *Instilling hope.* Research shows that psychologically healthy individuals put more focus on the future than on the past. The sign of a psychologically healthy individual is hope. A healthy group dynamic helps the client become more hopeful about the future. As group members put the insights they have gained into action, they become more hopeful and develop more faith in the therapeutic process. Hope is vital to recovery. Hope means that the person sees a brighter tomorrow and therefore has something to live for. Seriously depressed clients have little or no hope; if the group process can help instill hope, it has been beneficial.

    Psychiatrist Carl Jung explained that in the beginning of a group session the counselor has the person talk about "what happened to you" (the past), but in the end of the group the therapist is encouraged to ask "What are you going to do?" (turning the client to consider the future). This is to encourage the client to look hopefully to the future before leaving the therapeutic session. "It is not only the outlook but the uplook that counts."

4. *Universality.* Whether a person is male or female, black or white, young or old, wealthy or poor, people are far more the same than different. This understanding is often a by-product of group interaction. As the clients share with each other, they

learn that all generally have similar feelings, hopes and fears. One learns that feelings are universal.

5. *Altruism.* Altruism means unselfishness. Many group members find out that they can unselfishly help others. In the beginning of the group, members often feel inadequate and demoralized. As the members continue in the group, they realize that they can help and positively influence others and that their ideas and suggestions have value. This is a positive therapeutic effect.

6. *Interpersonal learning.* As members interact with others, they learn about the world and themselves. They may improve their social skills and problem-solving behaviors and develop a deeper understanding of others. Another aspect of interpersonal learning is developing an understanding (insight) of how others view them. The more individuals understand themselves and others, the more effective they can become.

7. *Imitative behavior.* Most psychologists believe that we learn the behaviors by imitating others. Hopefully, we learn positive behaviors in group counseling. As the members watch each other, they learn to model more effective behaviors. They learn from each other.

8. *Corrective recapitulation of the primary family.* Everyone has a need for acceptance and love. Everyone has unresolved family problems. With the breakup of the nuclear family the research shows an increase in distrust and distress. Research shows that a child suffers more five years after a parental divorce than right after the divorce. An effective group takes on the role of a family in which the member can resolve issues that were not overcome as a child. Since group members may come from dysfunctional families, the group can demonstrate how a functional family operates. Hopefully these positive behaviors carry over into the client's interpersonal life. The most important emotion that a person can learn from group counseling is caring and love.

9. *Group cohesiveness.* In some families and workplaces loyalty and dedication are decreasing. As the group members become more bonded, the closeness of the group improves each one's self-acceptance, esteem, respect, and love for others. This learning of affection is important for the client to develop healthy relationships outside the group. "Pick your friends, but not to pieces."

Essential Guidelines for Groups

1. *Group Participants.* Generally the literature suggests groups that work best are heterogeneous (Slavenson, 1947), meaning that they have a variety of different members. (i.e. males and females, different ethnic groups, diverse ideas, beliefs, and attitudes). Obviously a homogeneous group of severely depressed people might talk its members into deeper depression.

    There are times, however, that homogenous groups are advantageous. For example, many women feel hindered to discuss their problems if men are present and therefore benefit from an all women's group. Bach (1954) also suggests that it is not helpful to mix young with older adults or senior citizens if the topic is sexual experiences. Homogeneous groups for certain types of problems (drugs, alcohol, and sex) also have proven effective.

    Additionally, Hobbes (1951) and Bach (1954) identified populations who do not fit well with groups and often should be excluded because they could ruin group cohesion. They include:

    a. People that have psychological sophistication, but they use it to treat others cruelly.
    b. Severely aggressive or hostile people, who can destroy the freedom and acceptance among the group members.
    c. People who know each other well outside the group. This includes relatives.
    d. People who are psychotic or have an insufficient contact with reality (lacking of insight)
    e. People who talk too much and may monopolize the group.
    f. People with antisocial personalities or who are highly impulsive and hostile.
    g. Paranoid individuals, because they blame everyone else in the group, but themselves.
    h. Severely psychotically depressed or schizophrenic individuals.
    i. People who are extremely critical individuals.
    j. Narcissistic people, who egocentrically only care about themselves.

    k. People who destroy the group's trust by taking information out of the group or using information learned in the group against the person.

As this is not an exhaustive list, there are obviously other individuals that may not do well in groups. SEW has found that many of these clients when put into a large Sensitivity Group often get caught up in the atmosphere and lay aside their pathologies, which can bring about dramatic changes. However, if the individual has severely imbedded personality traits and a small group leader is in doubt about that client, she can put the person into the group until he does not work well, at that point she can remove him. While an ideal group is desired, the realities of agencies often dictate that everyone should be in a group. However, you can have advanced groups for highly motivated clients, and retain the destructive group member in a remedial group or individual counseling. As a result, the more productive and motivated clients will benefit more from the advanced group. When clients in the remedial group change personality characteristics to a more therapeutic bent, they can graduate into the advanced group. Regardless of the present state of the client, it must remain the challenge for all counselors to find ways to reach all clients.

2. *Size of group.* Generally the ideal group size for adults is between six and ten people. (Gazda 1970). In too large a group, a person can get bored and feel ignored. Corey (1985) suggests that children's groups be as small as three to four because of children's greater need for attention. Realistically, however, because of the tremendous need for groups and the lack of trained counselors to run them, groups can become enormous. Agencies find larger groups to be more cost effective; therefore, they are often far above the optimal size. One suggestion, for larger groups is to employ more interns or co-leaders to help facilitate the group or to be used to form subgroups. If that is not possible, the counselor can train motivated clients to help run the group.

Because large group sizes are very common, counselors have to use many creative ways to run groups. Forming sub-groups and having clients pair up with each other remain alternatives to larger groups.

When one counselor is running a large group, he might resort to lecturing its members; this approach is not therapy.

3. *Adding new members*: The concern becomes "open versus closed" groups. The ideal is to start a new group, close it to new members, and continue this group for the allotted time. This closed group tends to build family atmosphere with trust and intimacy.

    Reality, however, often dictates that most groups be open to new members. This becomes a controversial issue because new members can impact on the trust of the group. Also, adding new members complicates the orientation and adjustment problems of the new member and takes away from the deeper dynamics developed by the established members.

    Often, the solution to open groups is having graduated groups, where the more open and honest individual earns the right to enter an advanced group. This can occur when a clinician with a large caseload, such as in a therapeutic community, is required to conduct therapy sessions. The counselors can divide the group members according to their levels of cooperation, commitment and honesty.

4. *Frequency and length of a group*. Generally most outpatient groups meet once per week. Some agencies concurrently have some clients seeing counselors privately, once or more times per week, depending upon the seriousness of the issue. Usually the longer in weeks the group runs, the more trust and cohesiveness the group develops, especially if the members hold to the concept of confidentiality and are supportive of each other. The length of time for each group is about one and a half to two hours.

Generally, the literature suggests if the group is larger, the group must be run longer. The obvious problem of running groups longer is that group members can become bored, sleepy, agitated, annoyed and disruptive. The literature suggests that older clients do better than younger clients in longer groups. However, when groups are kept lively, interactive, and interesting, groups can be run for a longer period of time. Many of our groups run up to six or seven hours long and yet the main criticism of these groups is that the groups are too short.

5. *Rules of the Group.* In the beginning of every group, after the
    group members identify themselves, it is vital that everyone
    be crystal clear about the rules of the group. Because of their
    particular backgrounds, some members of the group have high
    levels of distrust. Being clear about rules will reduce the distrust
    and help clients be more open to each other. There are seven
    rules to stress over and over. They are:

    a. *Confidentiality.* "Whoever gossips to you, will be a gossip of
        you." Clients are encouraged to say in unison, "Whatever is
        said in the group stays in the group." Confidentiality is often
        a group member's greatest concern because they all have
        "secrets" that they would not like others to gossip about.
    b. *No judging.* "People who try to whittle you down are only trying
        to reduce you to their size." The members are encouraged to
        say, "I will not judge you and I don't want you to judge me."
        It should be made clear that group members are not judges,
        but part of the healing process. No one likes to feel as if
        others are rejecting him or her because of secrets the client
        has brought to light.
    c. *No observers (total participation).* Everyone in the group is
        encouraged to participate and not just be a spectator. Even
        group leaders are encouraged to appropriately self-disclose.
        Sometimes group members think a quiet non-self disclosing
        group member is just listening to get information to gossip
        about. Group members may feel rejected if a group member
        is not responding positively to them.
    d. *No sidelining.* Sidelining consists of group members holding
        private conversations while the group is in session. Group
        members often see this behavior as disrespectful. Attention
        must remain focused on the speaker.
    e. *No sleeping.* Sleeping in a group is disrespectful to the group,
        and the sleepy person should have group pressure from others
        to wake up and share or to leave the group. When a person
        wants to be in the group but is too sleepy encourage the
        member to stand, stretch or use cold water on his or her face.

f. *Total, brutal, and complete honesty.* This is a very important rule because group members feel betrayed if the person has them believing lies. It is unhealthy for members to lie and manipulate because it covers up the therapeutic issues that the client needs to expose.

g. *Only one person leaves the room at a time.* Sometimes in small group several people go to the bathroom all at once. People are told to use the bathroom before and after the group. If the groups are unusually long, the members could be given a break in the middle. It is important to stress that no walking in and out of the group is permitted. This behavior often makes a person that is using the group feel rejected.

h. *Land the plane.* In any group there are some people who like to talk too much and can monopolize a group so others can't share. The group leader suggests that if any person doesn't get to the "point" or takes too much time, then the leader will say "land the plane" as a signal for that participant to finish up and share the time with others.

Many groups also prohibit (and should prohibit) socializing outside of the group and especially having sexual relations with another group member. If two members of the group are having an affair with each other, they are not likely to open up about their deepest, darkest issues because they will be spending too much time trying to impress their paramour.

Other logistical rules of the groups are often No Smoking, No Violence, No Cursing, Be Respectful of Other Members, No Eating, No Chewing Gum, Be Prompt, and Stay for the Entire Group. Generally, it is best to develop rules of the group initially so that the members will own the rules. If someone consistently breaks the rules later the group members will bring social pressure on the person, which makes compliance more likely. If a group member refuses to abide by these rules, the person could be voted out of the group.

Again, stress over and over the importance of No Judging. To illustrate, in a Secrets Group, a woman may share that she is afraid to sleep in the dark. If a male youth giggles at that weakness, the woman closes up. While the secret may have tickled the youth's machismo, our psychotherapeutic senses are tickled wondering what event caused this woman to be afraid of the dark. That misplaced giggle has submerged the secret yet again. Therefore, a group leader who observes a person taking another person's issues lightly should remind the group members of the No Judging rule. In another example, a person who has perpetrated a crime, e.g., rape, could be reflexively judged by a member who has suffered such a crime. Group members need to be reminded that perpetrators need to be healed too, especially so that they do not repeat their crimes. However, it is important that a victim refrain from judging the perpetrator in the middle of his confession.

Additionally, clients are encouraged to talk about what they did, not what they would never do. For example, if a client says, "I would never take drugs or abuse somebody," it could shut down a person who was on the verge of just confessing to such a serious shame issue.

Finally, stress that trust is a very important principle and rules create boundaries about trust. Of course, rules vary from group to group, but if confidentiality is not kept then the trust of the group is sacrificed. If a group member is caught gossiping about someone else's problem outside of the group, she is confronted by the group. If one persists, she can be taken out of the group and seen individually. In therapeutic communities, a member that seriously breeches confidentiality can be rejected from the program.

While confidentiality between participants is vital, it behooves the group counselors and therapists to be familiar with HIPPA laws. The HIPPA laws are quite clear about when confidentiality must be breached.

1. Confidentiality must be breached when someone clearly seems motivated to harm another person. For example, if a client says he is going to kill his ex-girlfriend, it is the responsibility of the counselor to either talk him out of it, or if not successful at that, the therapist must alert the woman of his intentions. If he can't find the woman, the therapist must alert the police.
2. Confidentiality must be breached when a client is talking about harming himself or herself (suicide). Again the counselor should do all he can to try to save the client's life, or notify authorities.
3. Confidentiality must be breached in cases of child or elder abuse. When there is clear evidence of abuse, the counselor is required to report the abuse to the proper authorities.

It is not a breach of confidentiality if clinical staff discuss each client in a staff meeting, but the meeting must be confidential.

CHAPTER 5

Group Leaders

Ability will enable a man to go to the top, but it takes
character to keep him there.

—Anonymous

Corey and Corey (1987) in a careful study identified the thirteen characteristics of an effective group leader as follows:

1. *Courage.* The group leader is captain of the ship and remains in charge at all times. Obviously, if the ship is in a storm, and the captain becomes irrational and cowardly, the crew falters and mutiny is more likely. The group leader needs to know that the group will not usually force him into an uncomfortable situation as long as the leader shows courage. It is important that a group leader is experienced and knowledgeable or the group can degenerate into a free for all.

2. *Willingness to model.* "The most valuable gift you can give another is a good example." Group leaders need to be open and to be able to drop their masks or their images. If the group leader is demonstrating role modeling in a psychodrama, he should be able to drop his persona and actually demonstrate an issue in his own life, and do this with confidence. A group leader can only take a group as far as he has gone himself. If the group leader is not willing to drop his persona, his image, how can he expect the group members to do it? Clearly, a group leader

needs to be a good role model, not only inside the group, but in his personal life as well.

3. *Presence.* "Authority makes some people grow and others just swell." When one walks into a group, a person should be able to easily identify the group leader. A good leader is not a control freak, but must garner the respect and deference of the group. Effective leaders should have last say in the group. The delicate balancing act of control and charisma develops with experience, sometimes years in the making, for most group leaders. One of the ways that a group leader gains this respect and loyalty is through asking questions, knowing names, and listening intently. "You can win more friends with your ears than with your mouth." A good memory is vital, and accurate feedback from a leader can demonstrate that the leader was listening and trying to understand. Respect and loyalty are earned and cannot be demanded.

4. *Goodwill and caring.* "Those who bring sunshine to the lives of others cannot keep it from themselves." Possibly the most important characteristic that a group leader needs to impart is goodwill and caring. Since one of the deepest cravings of a person is to feel loved, a group leader needs to show he cares. One goal of a leader is to teach the members to love each other and to care sincerely for each other. As a group member shares, each should treat the client's story as a gift to be received. The group leader teaches deep caring by holding the client's self-disclosures in awe and teaching other group members to do the same. If a female shares being the victim of a severe, violent sexual attack and is weeping deeply, the group leader rallies the group in empathetic listening. When she is finished, the members are encouraged to group-hug her. Any other members who have had similar experiences are urged to self-disclose and help her feel that she is not alone in this issue. One of the most important aspects of the healing process is telling your story in an accepting atmosphere where compassion is evident and sincere.

5. *Belief in the group process.* If a group leader looks at running this group as a job or as a way to get a paycheck, eventually the members will catch on and lose respect for this individual. Often, group leaders that are discouraged and turned off from

running groups are individuals that are either afraid of their own therapeutic issues or are burned out because of overwork, stress, or a sense of failure. They have become disheartened many times by clients that have "failed" or dropped out. When this occurs, the group leader then needs his issues worked on before he can return to the group process effectively. The group leader must believe that the group process will work or a self-fulfilling prophecy of doom will ensue and the leader's unconscious belief can backfire in his face.

6. *Openness.* Often a leader has his or her own biases. When a client shares a sincere story with the group, the leader must be on guard that the flow of the story is not being prejudiced by the leader's own filters of gender, race, language, and religion. The story needs to flow easily into the large listening space provided by the group, and the story needs to be accepted with the caring and acceptance expressed above.

7. *Nondefensiveness and coping with attacks.* "Too many counselors quit looking for work when they find a job." Since leaders are the focal point of the group, clients may launch judgments, biases, and wrongs upon him or her everywhere from the lack of a haircut to the color of a tie. Group leaders may appreciate the attention they receive, but should not get hooked into the negative responses they may feel. For example, one female leader running a group related that a female member shouted out, "Do you know we can see through your dress?" Clients will ask, "How much do you make? What is your motivation for being here? What do you know about my life? How can you help me?" Since counselors can only take a client as far as they have gone themselves; this is where the rubber meets the road. When a client starts attacking a counselor on issues that the counselor has not resolved, the counselor may reflexively become defensive.

A counselor needs to have worked on his or her own therapeutic issues before attempting to run groups. It is vital that the counselors know what it is like to be a client, so that they can identify with what clients are going through. Some of the least effective counselors are ones who have never been in therapy themselves. This is why group leaders encourage interns and volunteers to use the group if a therapeutic issue comes up for them. Some of the best group leaders that have come out of SEW processes have been the clients who have "been there and done that." They have graduated out of the ashes of a destructive lifestyle. When these former clients say, "I can identify. I have been there," their statements are genuine.

8. *Personal power.* The group leader must be the most powerful person in the group, but must also earn that power, through gaining the trust and the respect from the group members. This is difficult for a group leader to learn. Each leader must work on gaining power through his or her own personal resources.

9. *Stamina.* Group leaders have to first take care of themselves. Obviously, if the group leader does not have the energy to invest in the group, the members may feel that the leader does not care and/or lose respect for the leader. Leaders should schedule their groups to their convenience and not at times when they might be tired and fatigued.

10. *Willingness to seek new experiences.* "Man cannot discover new oceans unless he has the courage to lose sight of the shore." Many orthodox methods are available in psychotherapy books. However, people are more complex than one theory can encompass. Sometimes, group leaders are too rigid in their orthodoxies. They may need to cast aside their obsessive-compulsiveness and keep their minds open. Often the groups that have most engrossed members have been those groups where the leader has been experimenting with a new method. The leader's investment in the group is at a much higher level than those groups that use a rigid formula. One way to improve groups is by listening to the participants who make suggestions and trying out those suggestions. Whether they work or fail, taking clients' suggestions helps the client to make a greater investment in the group.

11. *Self-awareness.* "Your words are windows to your heart." When a clinician does not know who she is, she is not going to be able to help a client know who he is. One way to find out about one's self is to attend groups regularly. Groups give much feedback about who a person is. Cherish this self-awareness. It helps a person grow. When one is honest and open in a

group, usually groups are not as ominous and as frightening. One exercise to develop self-awareness is to take a hand mirror and meditate staring into the mirror for five minutes. While the belief in our physical shortcomings is immense, this five-minute meditation helps with learning to know and accept ourselves. When we did this exercise, we became first aware and second quite enamored of our graying temples and our crow's-feet eyes. We recognized the experience that was inherent in these signposts. No longer did we feel we had lost it, but rather we had found the beauty of our years. What a valuable lesson to accept ourselves!

12. *Sense of humor.* "Humor is to life what shock absorbers are to automobiles." When working in a psychiatric hospital on a maximum-security ward with paranoid clients, Dr. Coleman had to be very careful not to laugh or tell jokes to the other attendants. When a new and naïve attendant would come on the ward, laughing and telling jokes, inevitably the paranoid client would think the attendant was talking about him and would become belligerent toward that attendant. Usually group members are not nearly as touchy as patients on a psychiatric ward, but we all have feelings. A sense of humor needs to be appropriate and not at a client's expense. Many scientific studies clearly suggest that humor is very healthful for the body.

   Often toward the end of a session, a counselor can use appropriate humor to lighten up the atmosphere and help clients transition back into post-group everyday life. A counselor needs to be cheerful and upbeat and learn to laugh at herself, but must be very careful about laughing about other people.

13. *Inventiveness.* This concept means being able to think on one's feet. If a standard technique doesn't seem to be working, one could tweak it a little bit and come up with a more novel approach that might work. There must always be a certain open-endedness to each group processes. Be in touch with one's creativity. When one is in a dynamic of different personalities, holding to rigid notions can be self-defeating for a group leader. The leader needs to be flexible and bend according to the currents flowing within the group. New, more therapeutic, and invigorating ideas

have arisen out of the jelling of several minds together in the group dynamic.

While it is obviously a tall order to have all of these characteristics, this list can challenge us to grow to be more effective and flexible. A counselor should look at the group interaction as a growing process, not only for the members, but also for herself. Over many years we have watched counselors and psychologists fresh out of graduate school sit in groups with their traditional orthodoxies learned in graduate school without an underlying grounding of "street smarts" or "group smarts." We have watched groups slowly turn on the counselor. Because the counselor does not understand or is not able to work with the group dynamic, the counselor often becomes embittered, defensive, and so often gets burned out and lashes back or flees. The purpose of this book is to help an ethical and honest group leader reach the pinnacle of his or her effectiveness.

Group Leaders and Coleaders

It is ideal to have at least one leader and one coleader in each group. In that manner one leader can run the group and the other can observe what is happening. The leader and coleader can take turns running the group if they are both following the same goals and practices. A group leader can offer continuity and step in when the coleader is distracted or called away from the group (late, sick, on vacation, etc.). Also, if a group member has an emergency (e.g., panic attack) one leader can take the distressed person outside of the group and administer to his needs without disrupting the group (Ritter, 1982). Coleaders may be interns or persons in training. This is an excellent way to train future leaders when interns cannot be found for coleaders. It can be helpful for leaders to train veteran group members to become coleaders. This approach is often seen as inspiring to other group members. Additionally, group leaders could recruit outside volunteers from the community to help run groups. To bring different perspectives to a group is encouraged. Embrace diversity and diplomacy wherever possible. Mix up leaders and coleaders, such as if a leader is female, the coleader is male. Or if the group leader is African American have a coleader of another ethnic origin. It doesn't seem to matter what gender the group leader is, it is the leader's skill that counts (Pietrofesa, et al. 1984).

It is recommended that coleaders sit opposite each other, so that they can have a complete view of the group. A group leader cannot see body language of group members that are sitting next to him, but a coleader on the opposite side of the group could bring it to the leader's attention. Sometimes, there will be rivalries and conflicts between group coleaders. They must be carefully resolved before the group starts. Certain minor conflicts between coleaders can be resolved in front of the clients to teach them cooperation skills. But serious conflicts between group leaders should be aired behind closed doors, so that when the leaders run the group, they demonstrate a "unified front" to the group (Dinkmyer and Muro, 1979). Serious conflicts between coleaders can be similar to mothers and fathers arguing in front of the children. It is disruptive to the group process and not found to be therapeutic.

Leadership styles. "The only fool bigger than the person who knows it all is the person who argues with him." Two important qualities that leaders of groups must achieve are respect and cooperation. These intangible qualities must be earned, not demanded. In studying a large number of group styles, Yalom et.al. (1971) found that authoritarian leaders (those that were highly controlling and confrontational) caused group members to be very defensive, passive, resentful, afraid, and less open—obviously not a highly therapeutic atmosphere. At the other end of the perspective, *laissez-faire* leaders (those that set few boundaries and took no control over the group itself, letting the group do whatever it chose) had the least effectiveness and the most number of group "casualties." Many times *laissez-faire* groups degenerate into vicious encounter sessions where the hostility factor of angry members surfaces and alienates other group members. Effective group leaders must find a middle ground between control and no control. Yalom also explained that expressing anger in group is good, but too much of it is harmful. Love, warmth, and support are most important to the group process. There should be a balance between feeling and thinking. They are both important to a productive group. However, group process is far more interested in feelings because thinking can sometimes degenerate into rationalization and intellectualization and be counterproductive.

Brutal Honesty. The final extremely important quality for group leaders is to be *totally, completely, and brutally honest*. Everyone uses defense mechanisms and as a result has difficulty relating to unvarnished honesty. As the group progresses, participants need to learn complete honesty and not be afraid that someone will laugh at them or put them down or judge them. Once the leaders can achieve complete honesty *in the right atmosphere*, the healing of a broken heart really starts to take effect. It becomes the task of the group leader to create an atmosphere that is safe and conducive for the group members to be totally, brutally frank and honest with themselves within the group setting. If the atmosphere becomes like a locker room, where self-disclosure is used against the person and people make cruel jokes about painful issues that are brought up, then sincere individuals will resist coming to the group. It is extremely vital that group leaders, with the help of the group, establish clear boundaries.

Effective group leadership requires courage, talent, and patience. Good leaders evolve. A group leader's attitude should manifest the following:

THE SHIP THAT SAILS

I'd rather be the ship that sails
And rides the billows wild and free;
Than to be the ship that always fails
To leave its port and go to sea.

I'd rather feel the sting of strife,
Where gales are born and tempests roar;
Than to settle down to useless life
And rot in dry dock on the shore.

I'd rather fight some mighty wave
With honor in supreme command;
And fill at least a well-earned grave,
Than die in ease upon the sand.

I'd rather drive where sea storms blow,
And be the ship that always failed
To make the ports where it would go,
Than be the ship that never sailed.
(Unknown)

CHAPTER 6

Objectives of Groups

What lies behind us, and what lies before us are tiny matters,
compared to what lies within us.
—Oliver Wendell Holmes

Numerous objectives for group therapy are similar to the requirements of being an effective group leader. Being honest, developing and maintaining trust, identifying accurate feelings, teaching love, and offering emotional healing requires much effort and experience.

Honesty: In group therapy, members are repeatedly told to be *totally, brutally, and completely honest.* Ramsey Clark said, "Honesty is the best policy in international relations, interpersonal relations, labor business, education, family, and crime control because truth is the only thing that worked and the only foundation on which lasting relations can build." In self-healing, honesty remains the most important ingredient. Psychologically speaking, it is the surgeon's thread and needle that is used in heart surgery to heal a broken heart. Total honesty is extremely painful and often is accompanied by copious tears. Therapists must consistently stress to clients—*no pain, no gain.* The more painful the issue, the more gainful the surgery. Most people are manipulative to some degree. Because members may erroneously believe that blaming games and projection are honesty, every client has got to be taught what honesty is. Clients need to keep the focus on self and how an environmental issue broke their hearts and how that felt. Clients are told to focus on personal issues and talk about their own secrets.

One saying that is repeated constantly is "You're only as sick as your secrets." The deeper the secret, the more painful the feelings. As a fungus grows profusely in the darkness, when brought to the light, it dies. Just so, secrets need to be brought to the light so that they lose their control on a person's life. To illustrate, one female client said she developed panic attacks when going out with a man that she desired and could see herself marrying. She said the thought of him even touching her caused her unbearable anxiety. She said she did not have a clue why she felt this way. In fact, she said she did not like any male touching her. After some lessons in relaxation techniques, she broke down in tears and confessed her secret. She was able to remember a frightening incident of sexual abuse in her childhood. The confession, associated with the relaxation and the confidence that she could cope with this anxiety, helped heal this boundary issue and ultimately opened the door to heal her broken heart and move ahead in her relationship. Without her secret being confronted, she could possibly have remained alone and not happily married. Her confession was redeeming, and her honesty was necessary for her healing.

Group Trust: Since clients may come from dysfunctional families one of the goals of a group is to create a "functional family" in therapy. Therefore, *group trust* becomes vital. Group members should be held in awe when they self-disclose, and the confidential nature of their confessions needs to be held sacred. And if taken out of the group, the group members must discipline the transgressor because discussing someone's secret out of group causes distrust.

Focus on Feelings: Groups are all about feelings. Psychologists suggest that we are a society of emotional reasoners. Media is constantly appealing to people's emotions. Emotional manipulation sells products. People buy more expensive name brand products and unnecessary goods because of the emotional appeal. Even though some of the time people can't trust their feelings, within a therapy group feelings must be acknowledged and validated. One way to do this is with several basic sayings:

There are no right or wrong feelings.
All feelings are valid.
Speak from your heart, not from your mind.

The group leader verbalizes, "*I want to know how you feel, not what you think.*" Often the thinking a group member presents is his persona or simply a rationalization. Since many, especially men, are given the message "Don't feel" by society, some persons have no idea how to identify and to express emotions. Whether feelings are rational or irrational, simply expressing the feelings, and feeling the feelings, e.g., crying, is so cathartic as to go a long way in healing a broken heart. As a result, the ability to feel pain is gainful in and of itself. We often spend our lives trying to avoid pain. This is what psychologists often call the *cosmic joke*. The cosmic joke really isn't funny, but goes like this, "The more we try to avoid the pain, the more pain we suffer." Addicts are consistently trying to numb their bodies by using Librium, Valium, and/or analgesics including morphine and heroin. Not many people in society suffer more pain, shame, guilt, and rejection than addicts. So the solution is to go after the pain, that is, heal your broken heart. Only then can one find joy. This, however, is very difficult to convince group members. It is just the opposite of what is learned in society. Who wants to confront painful issues? Everyone wants surgery to be pain-free. But that is not totally possible. Clients must be taught to get over their fear of pain, or therapy may become a meaningless, didactic exercise of complaining and blaming and whining and anger. Some people just want that pill to reduce the anxiety and don't want to go through the painful process to discover the root of the problem. When the client can be taught to dive into the pain, recovery is quicker and the anxiety and depression is left behind.

Teach Love: Some therapists believe that teaching love in a therapy group is inappropriate. They believe, instead, in teaching a type of caring called empathy. They say that teaching love gets a person too emotionally involved. Consider the opposite—teaching love is a primary goal of therapy.

Natural affection, as opposed to lust, teaches real caring. If the clients are taught to sincerely care for other group members, then they may sincerely want what is best for their group peers. One reason people are afraid to care is that love is painful. Loved ones can reject you, disappear, or die. But knowing how to heal a broken heart can lead to learning to love again. Being not afraid to face the pain, but being able to talk about it and to cry over it, can heal a broken heart. Remaining bitter is unhealthy. Healing is often a skill many people find difficult to achieve on their own; teaching healing should be a prime objective of groups. A group can demonstrate what a loving, functional family is like, so that members can use this skill outside the group, building functional families and loving relationships on their own.

CHAPTER 7

Helpful Hints in Running Groups

When you think you are looking bad, you are looking good,
When you think you are looking good, you are looking bad.
—Anonymous

Some clients are forced to attend groups by judges, family, or other authorities. If the clients are resistant to being there, the group can be difficult to conduct. When these clients are extremely resistant to treatment, it is often better that they be seen individually rather than be allowed to disrupt the entire group. When a resistant client becomes more accepting of therapy, he or she can later be transitioned back to the group. Until then, groups with eager participants can benefit from several principles.

One slogan that is repeated often in groups is *When you think you are looking bad, you are looking good, and when you think you are looking good, you are looking bad.* Give new group members a careful orientation of the rules and expectations, because clients become confused and don't understand the value of self-disclosure. It only takes one resistant member of a group to have a detrimental effect on the trust and openness of the whole group. For example, one could damage another group member by laughing or mocking the honesty and self-disclosure of another. Explain to the clients that groups are not for talking about the weather or other innocuous subjects. They are for talking about *guilt, shame, pain, conflict,* and *secrets.* Sometimes resistant clients will want to talk about what happened in the news instead of what has happened to *himself* and how he *feels.*

At first clients are naturally resistant to expressing feelings, but as they begin to see the relief that other clients get from expressing feelings, they begin to open up themselves. A therapist may say, "I want to know how you feel about this, not what you think about it." Often clients give their rationalizations or other defense mechanisms instead of talking about real feelings. For example, one woman explained that her father never told her that he loved her or expressed warm feelings toward her.

"How did that you make you feel?" the therapist inquired.

"It was okay, that is the way it was," she said, shaking her head dejectedly.

"That is your thinking; I want to know your feelings about him," the therapist replied.

"I hated it! I hated it!" she screamed, as tears began to stream from her eyes. "I believed he really hated me."

New clients may need to be taught the difference between feeling and thinking. When the clients first come to group they may distrust and fear the group members will gossip about them or laugh at them. Therefore a group leader says, "You came alone, and you will leave alone." This means that clients should not see other group members socially and might never see these people again after the group. Group leaders strongly discourage any sexual contact between clients. If a person is coming to group, thinking about physical or sexual attractions toward other group members, it often destroys the person's honesty and often disrupts the honesty of the other person as well.

One principle that group leaders strongly discourage is *blaming games*. Often clients take the focus off themselves by telling how others are to blame for their problems. Blaming takes the responsibility off the client and puts it on the person blamed. If the therapist, especially in a therapeutic community, allows the group to run itself, the discussion often degenerates into the client's complaining about a lousy counselor, bad food, or other blaming issues.

Another principle that should be identified is the definition of a *therapeutic issue*. A therapeutic issue is a refusal to accept something. For example, if you are angry at somebody because she rejected you, by definition, you have not accepted her rejection. This immediately causes a therapeutic issue. If a person was sexually abused as a child and repressed that memory, she is not accepting and working on this issue, and it often creates a personal problem.

Obviously people don't have to accept everything. If you have cancer, you first have to lift the denial and accept the fact that you have cancer. Then you get the best medical treatments to rid your body of this cancer. So acceptance is not the entire story. The sexually abused person must first accept the fact that they were abused, process it, and eventually overcome the issue. One of the wisest sayings to memorize is the Serenity Prayer. "May God grant me the serenity to accept the things I cannot change, the courage to change the things I can, and the wisdom to know the difference."

Lengthy discussions about what they are refusing to accept in their lives help these clients figure out what they have to continue to accept and what they have in their power to change. Refusal to accept something is denial, often called resistance. Resistance is a big word for *fear*, and *fear* is the biggest obstacle toward getting a person to accept something. Usually the resistance is a big paper tiger that looks terrifying, but is just a bunch of feelings that need to be expressed and certainly not as dangerous as they initially appear.

Another important slogan that is taught to clients is *the only person who can change you is yourself.* This saying expresses the point that we can only change ourselves and learn to adapt; but many times the more we attempt to change others, the more they resist change.

One approach for group cohesion and unity can occur when one member is talking about a particular painful experience (e.g., death of a loved one), and the leader asks the other group members to "raise your hand if you can identify with what this person has been through." When the client looks around the group and sees other hands raised and hears them say, "You are not alone," this helps the person realize how we are all connected by pain.

Finally, it is vital that the group leader know the members' names and uses those names often and encourages other group members to know each other's names as well. Dale Carnegie, in his book *How to Win Friends and Influence People*, explains that one of the most beautiful words that a person can hear is the sound of his or her own name. It makes a person feel important.

CHAPTER 8

The Journey Starts

Artists who seek perfection in everything are those who cannot attain it in anything.

—Eugene Delacroix

Knowing how to start a group, how to engage all members into the group process, how to make the group interesting, and how to prepare the members for the main group process moves the study of therapy from the theoretical to the practical. A new therapist sadly complained that he was looking for new group techniques in the literature. The therapist said that all the available books were full of theoretical material on processes, but none of the books put a "handle on how to really do the group." This therapist was very frustrated. Our attempt is a cookbook approach that is as specific as possible so that a therapist can follow these techniques and hopefully achieve effective results.

First, it is always advised to start the group (especially if there are new group members) with a member of the group explaining the group rules. Especially stress *confidentiality*. The member might have the group repeat "*Whatever is said in this group, stays in this group.*" Inform the group that strict *confidentiality* is a must, and anyone who is caught taking anything out of group must face other members who will confront that person and could vote that individual out of the group.

Next, the group needs ice breakers. Ice breakers are techniques that are designed to get group members awake, aware, motivated, and valuing the group. Our ice breakers are meant to be fun as well as to help members to value the group, to learn to relax, and to laugh with others. Listed below are many ice-breaking techniques.

Dancing

In many of our groups, especially if they have young people in them, we have the members dance. Young people love to dance. It helps them drop their images and be more secure about themselves and their bodies. One requirement is that males and females are not paired up; we use group dancing. If we do a soul train, we mix males and females in both lines. The only expectation that we have in this group dancing is that the clients are expected to make mistakes and that is okay.

One female client who attended many groups and eventually became a group leader said, "I used to be shy and I can't dance, but after many groups I still can't dance, but I am not shy anymore."

Paintbrush Technique

The most popular group dance is the paintbrush technique. In this dance several leaders stand in front of the group. The first person explains to the group that imaginary artistic blank canvases surround each group member. They make believe the canvas is in front of them, at the back of them, to the right, to the left, on the floor, and on the ceiling. It is also explained that an imaginary paint can is by each person's right foot. Group members are told that a part or parts of their bodies will become paintbrushes. The first group leader starts by using his right hand as a paintbrush. Some fast music is then played, and the members are encouraged to put their right hand (paintbrush) into a paint can and then paint on the imaginary canvas with that right hand. After they do this for a minute, the next person on the line might have the group put both hands (paintbrushes) into the paint can and then paint on the canvas in front, on the side, at the back, over the head. The next person in line might have the group put their head in the paint can, then their belly button, then paint around the canvas with their heads and bellybuttons. The next person might have the group members put their knees in the bucket and have them paint around with their knees. By this time the members are quite amused as the next group leader has the members paint with their various body parts. This exercise usually loosens up the group, helps participants lose their images and their masks, and helps achieve an uplifted, happy mood. If there are wallflowers in the group, this technique is very helpful in allowing them to come out of their shells because there are no exact movements that must be adhered to in this.

Relaxation

Relaxation, as previously demonstrated, is vital to reduce stress and to focus the person. Many clients come into group angry, depressed, anxious, or plain stressed out. Relaxation techniques calm down tempers, teach members how to reduce their blood pressure, calm their heart rates, and slow their metabolism so that while they are in the room they can fully participate in the ensuing group processes. Behavior therapists have used relaxation techniques such as systematic desensitization with great success for years.

One client said that previously he needed headphones blasting loud music to drown out the noises in his head. The client found that with relaxation through meditation, he was able to silence the unrelenting noises in his head.

Two relaxation techniques that are used together in group therapy are the "hold on, let go technique" and the "empty-bottle technique." During these exercises soft instrumental music is played in the background. The therapist talks to the group. The leader has the participants tense certain parts of their bodies until their entire bodies are tense. Then the leader has them hold on to that tension. As they tense their body, very intensely, the therapist has them make a loud sound to the tension they are feeling, making it louder, repeating this noise, and elevating the noise until they scream to the whole tension in their body. Then the leader has them fully relax. This process helps members start the relaxation, just like a tense person might feel relaxed after a jog.

The leader then systematically teaches the members to relax. The leader softly instructs. The meditation goes something like this:

Slowly, take a deep breath and imagine that your body is an empty bottle, so that when you inhale, the air not only goes to the bottom of your lungs, it also goes to the bottom of your toes, as it would if your body were an empty bottle. Just get the sensation that the air, when you breathe it in, is filling your body entirely, from the tips of your toes to the top of your head to the tips of your fingers. When you empty this bottle, by exhaling, your body becomes a vacuum for another breath that will fill your body totally with healing breath. So breathe in, fill this empty bottle, which is you, feeling yourself becoming more relaxed, and then breathe out and empty this bottle, which is you, breathing out anxiety and tension. As you are filling, and emptying this bottle, which is you, take a slow, careful inventory of your body and identify where you feel any tension, anxiety, discomfort, or pain. Don't do anything about that tension; just be aware of it. Continue to slowly empty and fill this bottle, which is your body, with healing, life-giving air.

After you have become aware of where the anxiety and tension is in your body, you then breathe in and let the air go to an area of your body that feels tense. Let it loosen up some of that tension, and imagine that tension being breathed out through your nostrils and gone forever. Again, as you breathe in, let the air go to an area of your body that feels tense, loosen that tension, breathe that tension out, and let that tension be gone forever. In this way, systematically relax your whole body of tension, anxiety, negative images, and anything else that prevents well-being. Loosen those negative feelings, breathe them out and, let them be gone.

The duration of this relaxation technique can be anywhere from thirty to forty-five minutes. Some members actually fall asleep in this meditation, which is okay. This often means they are fully relaxed. Usually, therapists should modulate their voice in order to keep the members active so that they do not fall asleep. (If you use a blood pressure cuff during this session, you will see a significant lowering of the blood pressure and heart rate over the process of this relaxation.)

There are other relaxation techniques that are effective. You can tense a particular body part one at a time and then relax it. Do this systematically all over the body and this too becomes helpful in teaching relaxation. We find, however, the empty-bottle relaxation technique most effective.

One word of caution: if you are starting out with a group that is fairly resistant to therapy, many times the members will simply use this time to take a nap and escape the group. You need to know your audience to know whether you should use this tool. For example, relaxation techniques do not work as well with resistant populations such as people involved with the correctional system.

Trust Exercises

"Do the thing you fear and the death of fear is certain." Most clients have a deep mistrust. As Erik Erikson suggests, the very first psychosocial stage a person enters has to do with trust versus mistrust. Many clients have learned distrust from childhood. This lack of trust issue translates to the questions "Are my needs being met? Can I rely on anybody?" One client related how his father stood him on a desk when he was four years old and told him to jump off while holding his arms poised as if to catch him. The boy jumped. The father removed his arms and let him crash to the floor. The father then said, "That will teach you a lesson. Do not trust anyone."

As a result the man had years of interpersonal problems because of his distrust of not only others but also himself. When the father said, "Do not trust anyone," his son included his own self as somebody not to be trusted. When a person distrusts others, he starts disliking the people he distrusts. He feels betrayed by them and believes his needs are not being met by them because, in reality, they are not being met. As this dislike for the person grows, this distrust can then get transferred to self. The adage "The more you dislike someone, the more you become like him" applies here. The individual starts acting distrustful because he thinks it is normal to do so. Trust exercises help regain the trust of self and others.

Trust exercises are helpful relationship builders and when executed correctly also effective ice breakers. Group dynamics texts give them in detail, and we simply mention some here. In one technique the leader has a group of eight to ten members stand in a circle, shoulder to shoulder around a single member, who is lying on his back on the floor. The member on the floor is asked to relax, as the other group members put their hands under the prone person's body, palms up. They then very slowly lift the individual until the person is lying above the group members' heads. They slowly rock that person and bring that person back down to the ground. The group leader then asks the member to describe how he felt as he was being levitated above the floor. The rest of the members of the group are all strongly encouraged to participate in this process.

Another trust exercise occurs when you blindfold a group member, put her in the middle of a circle of standing members, and have her walk directly ahead. Each circle member slowly touches the blindfolded person when she reaches him or her. The circle member gently turns and redirects the blindfolded one to continue to walk forward. This is done nonverbally. This helps the blindfolded one learn to trust that the group members will not play tricks and let them walk into a wall. Again, each member is encouraged to participate.

A similar trust exercise could be used by pairing up group members, blindfolding one of the pairs, and then having the other member lead them around the building, touching things and guiding them for ten minutes. Obviously, because it destroys trust if a member plays jokes on the blindfolded one, the group leader needs to monitor the crowd carefully.

Another trust exercise, called conveyor belt, should be done with only males. The group members form two parallel lines facing each other. Each line has its members touching shoulders, holding their hands out from the waist, palms up, almost touching the hands of the parallel line facing them. The group leader takes one person from the head of the line, leans them back on the hands of the members at the beginning of the conveyer belt, and lifts the member's feet. The members of the conveyor belt slowly and carefully pass the person down the line to the end, where another group leader places his arms under the person's armpits and carefully helps the person back to his feet. The person on the conveyor belt goes headfirst down the line, facing the ceiling. (If females are used in this process, they may not be strong enough to hold up heavy individuals. Additionally, going down the conveyor belt violates some women's sense of modesty.)

Finally, another trust exercise that has to be carefully monitored involves a safety net, such as a mattress on the floor. Have four people standing, two on each side of the mattress, arms interlocked. Have another member stand at the end of the mattress, with his back facing the mattress, and fall backward onto the arms of the four members. Sometimes the person stands on a chair as he falls backward. Never do this process without a mattress backup!

Songfest

"I loved the silliness of it. Singing made me feel like a regular person again," Sue Monk Kidd stated. Song is an ancient concept. Military marches, churches, celebrations, including funerals, employ music as a way to tie together emotions. William Congreve said, "Music hath charms to soothe the savage beast, to soften rocks or to bend a knotted oak." When members sing group songs, unity and positive feelings emerge. As an ice breaker, it may be helpful to give the clients the words, through supplying a visual copy, verbally rehearsing the words, or using a karaoke machine. If the group has talented individuals, they can croon their own songs and dazzle the group. Other times the whole group might stand in a circle, put their arms around the backs of the other members, and sing a group song, e.g., "You Are Not Alone," "Lean on Me," and "Can You Feel the Love Tonight." Care must be taken to use positive, uplifting, and spiritual songs.

Testimony

This ice breaker requires an articulate person who has had a psychological problem tell the group about his or her behaviors and issues. In the selection of a person to give a testimony, it is important to screen a person carefully so that the ten-to-fifteen-minute testimony can set a "therapeutic mood" for the other group members. Perhaps the one individual chosen to testify in groups had been sexually abused throughout his childhood and he can show how this abuse led to sexual and aggressive acting out in his own adulthood. Often testifiers start crying, and this helps other group members get in touch with their feelings and softens them up for talking about some of their deeper issues. When strict confidentiality is adhered to in the group, even new members can talk about some of their deepest issues without getting paranoid and regretting it later.

Bill, an ex-addict, explained to the group that he was sexually abused as a child by a man in the neighborhood, and later Bill allowed other boys to use him sexually because he wanted acceptance from others. Bill told the group that he had contracted AIDS and had thought that he was homosexual. After this admission from Bill, the other members of the group were more open and honest than usual. One member explained, "I was totally honest because after hearing Bill's testimony I realized that my problem wasn't all that severe after all." Testimonies can put individual circumstances into a different perspective.

The Yarn Process

In the yarn process, the group members form a large circle. The assistants hand the end of a skein of yarn to the first member and then walk around the circle with each member holding on to the yarn. The leader speaks about the unity of the circle and the yarn. If there is symbolism to the color of the yarn, e.g., red for health, blue for hope, the leader speaks to that. For instance, if in a recovery group the yarn color is blue, you would say, "Blue is for recovery. When you look at this yarn, you will remember the good feelings you had tonight, as blue is for remembering."

Ask the members to hold on to this yarn with their left hand, because the left hand is closest to their heart. Then the assistants take scissors and cut the yarn between each member. With the length of yarn left in each client's hand the assistants tie it around the client's wrist. The leader then explains that as long as the yarn bracelet remains on the client's wrist, the client is connected to the group. Many clients wear this yarn for weeks after the group. When they look at their yarn bracelets, this allows them to recapture the group's experiences and their individual growth.

Skits

Skits used in groups are designed to help clients relate to past issues. There are varying themes and different stories. The stories should be prepared ahead of time for the prospective audiences. When a group leader is adept, one can actually help a member spontaneously set up a real-life skit, which shares with the other members a past incident in his or her life.

One skit theme can be about an alcoholic abusive father. Use of seasonal holidays and themes can help when creating the skit. For example, one skit illustrates a father who arrives home drunk on Christmas Eve, with no presents for the children. When the children look for the tree and their presents, he beats them. Then the skit jumps to fifteen years later when one of the children is grown and returning home from being in a drug program. He confronts his father about the Christmas past. Since the holiday time is the worst for depression and unresolved psychological pain, this is a powerful skit to use during that season.

In a nonverbal skit, a young virgin is tempted by a suitor. She remains loyal to herself while her suitor tries various ways to seduce her. Eventually the man succeeds in stealing her heart and body, and then plays her for a fool. Until this point, all action has been nonverbally acted with the group mesmerized by the drama. The young girl starts to poignantly and audibly cry aloud. Her emotive wailing begins a chain reaction of tears from the spectators and serves as a powerful tool to help others get in touch with these feelings of betrayal and deception.

Tell the Group How You Feel

Telling the group how you feel is a very simple group starter. The leader asks each person to briefly tell how he or she feels right now. This gets the clients immediately involved and tells the group leaders who need to use the group first. This helps each member feel more connected to the group and more valued within the group. Also, an effective group leader learns how to get every member to share in every group.

Making the Rounds and Let Me Feed You a Sentence

In making the rounds the group is sitting in a circle. A member (person 1) is asked to rise from the chair and face the person next in line (person 2). Both members face each other standing. They hold hands and are instructed to make eye contact. The group leader then feeds the group, starting with person 1, a sentence. Looking into the partner's eyes, person 1 repeats what the leader said and then finishes the sentence. For instance, the leader might start "Right now I feel . . ." Person 1 might say, "Right now I feel anger at my wife for leaving me." Person 2 could state, "Right now I feel good because I am in group with my friends." Person 1 now sits and person 2 and person 3 now stand facing each other, holding hands and making eye contact. Person 2 would then face person 3. The group leader may feed this pair another statement or keep it the same. Person 2 would complete the statement to person 3, "Right now I feel . . ." until the entire group has completed this process at least once.

A therapist can feed a group member any kind of sentence starter. Listed below are a few popular ones:

> "Right now I wish . . ."
> "I love . . ."

"Right now I want . . ."
"I like . . ."
"My mother . . ."
"Do you know how I feel about you . . ."
"Do you know how I feel about myself . . ."
"I fear . . ."
"The thing that makes me anxious is . . ."
"I hate . . ."

Changing the sentence feed, or asking group members for sentence starter suggestions, is another way to get everyone alert and involved. Since one goal of a group is to have everyone in the group participate, this technique does so.

Do Something or Make a Noise

This is another simple ice breaker for the group. The leader asks each member to make a noise or do something that expresses how they feel right now. One person might jump up and down for joy, while another might scream at the top of their lungs. Another might moan or mope. Complete this activity until all members have participated.

Back Massage

Back massage is a real crowd pleaser. Since most people have skin hunger, this wakes up the entire group. In this activity the members count off by twos. The number twos stand in the back of the number ones and massage those persons' shoulders and neck. After a minute or two the parties switch.

Another back massage technique that can be used involves having the members stand in a circle. Each member turns, and faces right, and puts their hands on the person in front of them to massage their shoulders. This allows everyone in the group to get a massage at the same time. Sometimes, the group leader may need to show simple massage techniques.

Image Breakers

In this process group members write funny chores on a sheet of paper and put them in a box. Each member (including the leader) draws one out, reads it, and acts it out. Examples of image breakers are: Act like a chicken, pretend that you have to go to the toilet and that the stall is occupied, pretend to ask a member of the opposite sex out on a date knowing that you will be refused, pretend you are driving to a toll booth and have no money, pretend to lay an egg, pretend you are eating a distasteful meal, pretend you are a piece of bacon frying on a skillet, etc. See how many other funny image breakers you can think of. You can use the same image breakers in future groups. As the groups become closer, you can have a member act out an image breaker and have the other members guess what they are acting out. Usually the members are asked to act out the image breakers nonverbally.

Pair up and Discuss a Topic

In this simple procedure, group members are assigned or find a partner. Each pair is then given a topic to discuss. Again, stress the importance that everything that is discussed with the partner is totally and absolutely confidential. Some suggestions for discussion include: my earliest memory, my mother or my father, a secret I never told anyone, my worst experience or my best experience, the people I have loved and what happened to them, my most painful memory, someone who hurt me, someone who I hurt, things that I fear.

Since some clients may be too intimated by talking in front of large groups, pairing up will encourage the shy ones to open up more and be more honest. This simple process helps lure extremely shy members out from behind their protective wall. Additionally, this pairing can help a person improve social and listening skills.

Blow Faults into a Balloon

Every member is given a balloon and is asked to name a fault that they have. For each fault that is confessed, they are told to blow this fault into a balloon. After the balloon is blown full, the members let them go free and jet around the room. This is to help participants realize that they can let go of their faults. The balloons are then discarded and destroyed.

Imitate Someone in the Group

In this process, a volunteer is asked to act like someone in the group, and other members are asked to guess who that member is. The one who guesses can then act like someone else in the group. Obviously, this only works when group members have been together for some weeks and know each other. Also the group must be quite cohesive as this process might alienate members who are witnessing themselves being acted out. On the other hand, this often increases a person's awareness of how he or she may act, walk, talk, and relate to others.

Jane, a group member, was very grumpy and judgmental and always put a damper on the group process. After Maria imitated her, Jane instantly realized how she was acting. Her transformation started toward being a more positive and pleasing person.

The Clap Technique

The clap technique helps to create an alert, attentive audience. Often when teachers find their grade school classes out of order, they just stand very quietly in the front of the class. Likewise, to bring a group of people to attention a person may silently stand in front of the group. He puts his finger over his mouth to suggest that the group be quiet. When the group is quiet, the clap technique is initiated. The leader claps his hands once and looks expectantly at the audience. The leader does not say a word throughout this entire exercise. He simply looks to the audience and initiates a series of clapping sequences. Some members catch on and answer back with a clap. Then maybe the leader might clap twice and eventually the audience will clap back twice. The leader will clap three times and the audience will clap back three times. Again, the leader does not say a word.

In pantomime, just by pointing, the leader divides the room, perhaps into three parts, faces one group, and claps twice. After they respond with two claps, the leader faces the second group, claps twice, and that group will respond with two claps. Then the leader will repeat the two claps for the third group, and the third group will clap twice. He will then go back to the first group, then the second group, and so one. He will continue in this manner until the entire audience is involved.

There are variations to this clap technique; the leader may clap once when the group is expecting the presenter to clap three times, or the leader may have the first group clap once, the second group clap twice, and the third group clap three times. Sometimes people goof up, which causes laughter and levity. By the end of the clap technique, the group leader has the whole group's attention riveted on him.

"With These Hands I Have"

Each member within the group is successfully asked to repeat and complete this sentence "With these hands I have . . ." Starting with the group leader and going to the person on the right, this phrase-completion exercise keeps going round and round until the group leader tells the group to stop. A person might say, "With these hands I have done sexual things." Another might say, "With these hands I have gotten into fights." "With these hands I have done things that I feel very guilty about." "With these hands I have held my baby." "With these hands I have created art." "With these hands I have repaired engines." This exercise can continue for up to fifteen minutes. Each person may have to respond up to ten or fifteen times until this ice breaker is finished. If there is a trust exercise in the group, members often reveal guilt and shame that they are hiding. Each time the member's turn occurs, the statements usually become deeper and the group members bond more closely.

Group Scream

An initial exercise to help obtain cooperation from the group may start with a group scream. The group shouts, "You hurt me" ten times and then "I Love You" ten times. Daniel Cassriel in his book, *A Scream Away from Happiness*, explains how a group scream is done. The group members hold hands, and the group leader screams as loudly as he can, then squeezes the hand of the person to the right, and that person screams as loudly as she can, and then squeezes the hand of the person on her right, and the person on her right and round and round the circle until it comes back to the leader. Then the entire group will scream three times together. Sometimes the group leader will have the members scream a variety of phrases such as "I Love You," "I Hate You," and "You Hurt Me" over and over again as loudly as they can.

This method is also known as "priming the pump" because the screaming prepares the members for deeper processes that follow. At times the scream therapy can be incorporated into the whole group session. For example, after the initial scream, the group leader may look around the group and identify a member who seems to be "full of feelings."

"Miguel, how are you feeling right now?" asks the leader.

"I am angry," Miguel, an addict who relapsed over the breakup with his fiancée, states.

"You seem angry!" the group leader reflects.

"Yes, I am ferocious," Miguel says, sitting up defiantly.

"Now hug a pillow and scream 'I am angry' over and over," the group leader suggests as he walks behind Miguel and places his hands on Miguel's shoulders for support.

"I am angry! I'm angry, I'M ANGRY . . ."

"Louder! Scream louder! I can't hear you," the leader yells.

"I'M ANGRY! I'M ANGRY," Miguel yells even louder. Miguel stops, and tears well up in his eyes.

"What are you feeling right now?" the leader asks kindly.

"I feel hurt that she broke off with me and I don't know why."

"What is her name, Miguel?"

"Mary."

"Talk to her and tell her how you feel," the leader coaches.

"Mary, why did you leave me?" Miguel whispers.

"Louder," demands the leader.

'WHY DID YOU LEAVE ME?" Miguel yells over and over.

"Tell her how it makes you feel."

"It hurts. IT HURTS . . ." Miguel screams through his tears.

After Miguel has sobbed deeply and screamed his feelings out, group members get up and hug him and tell him they are proud of him for expressing real feelings. Miguel expressed at the end of the group that he felt as if a huge load had been lifted from his back Eventually, Miguel was able to regain his sobriety and take back his life.

Recite a Story or a Poem

Many times members have written poems or stories. Good ice breakers are to have the person read a personal story or recite a poem. Given the opportunity to share one's original pieces helps the member to invest more fully in the group and can help others to be more open as well.

Identify with an Animal

People often identify with attributes and behaviors of a particular animal. In this process, the members are asked to imagine an animal they believe is most like them. For instance, someone might choose a horse (because she feels like a workhorse), or a labrador retriever (because he is friendly). The members tell which animal they are and then act out the behaviors of that animal. This is done to music. This portrayal both is animated and fun as well as an insightful image breaker.

Letter Writing and Journaling

Each group member is asked to write a letter to a significant person in his or her life. The members may write to someone they love, or have loved, a parent, a child, a benefactor, or an offender; they may also write to themselves. In this letter the person asks for forgiveness or confesses a past wrongdoing. The members then read the letter to the group. Often addicts write a letter to a family member. When the family members are invited to join the group, the letter writer is asked to present this written confession to the family with soft music playing in the background. When these confessions are made, there are many tears.

Songs that are chosen to be played as background music often relate to the person's topic. Sometimes people are encouraged to sing it before reading, or it is played softly in the background. For example, use "It's So Hard to Say Goodbye" by Boyz II Men before the reading to a deceased person. Or "Song to Mama" by the same group before reading a letter to mother, and/or if it is a letter to Dad, use "Dance with my Father" by Luther Vandross.

Significant mental and physical benefits are attributed to journal and letter writing. Claudia Calb (1999) states,

> Professional writing has been around at least since the Renaissance. But new research suggests that it is far more therapeutic than anyone ever knew. Since the mid 1880's studies have found that people who write about their most upsetting experiences, not only feel better but also visit doctors less and even have stronger immune systems. More recently, doctors reported findings that made the link even clearer. A study published in the

Journal of the American Medical Association (*JAMA*) showed that writing exercises can help alleviate symptoms of asthma and rheumatoid arthritis. "It is hard to believe," says James Pennebaker, a psychology professor at the University of Texas at Austin and a pioneer in the field of expressive writing, "but being able to put experiences into words is good for your physical health. Letters do not have to be sent. You can always write to yourself in a journal. Psychotherapists say that journal keeping can be a powerful adjunct to traditional talk therapy."

The Laughing Process

"At the height of laughter the universe is flung into a kaleidoscope of new possibilities" (Jean Houston). If the intent is to create a happy atmosphere in the room, use contagious laughter. With laughter comes levity and release of negative feelings. Ask members to quietly think of something from their past that is funny. Wait for a member or two to start laughing. Attempt to involve everyone in the room. Often if the group leader laughs, others will follow. Soon laughter can spread throughout the room. Encourage the laughter.

Whispered Comments

In this process one member of the group is blindfolded and set in a chair in the middle of the circle of other members. The moderator stands outside the circle and puts an ear up to a person in the surrounding circle. That person whispers a comment to the moderator about the person sitting in the middle of the group. Then the moderator repeats to the person in the middle of the group the information that was given. For example, the moderator might repeat, "You are a friendly person."

The comments are requested to stay positive. If the moderator is told a fault of the blindfolded person, that comment might be restated to be helpful, rather than hurtful. For example, the moderator might alter the comment to target a specific behavior. Instead of saying, "You act stupid," the blindfolded person might be suggested to "Think more carefully before you do things." In other words, make a constructive suggestion for improving behavior.

The Twenty-dollar Bill Process

Have the members reflect on the value of a new crisp twenty-dollar bill. Members pretend they are holding a twenty-dollar bill. After a few minutes, members are then asked to imagine they are crumpling up their clean new twenty-dollar bill. Next members pretend they are throwing the twenty-dollar bill on the floor and crushing it under their feet and getting it dirty. Finally they pick up the crumpled, dirty twenty-dollar bill, and the group leader asks, "How much is this twenty-dollar bill worth now?"

Members respond that it is still worth $20, even if it is dirty and crumpled. The leader replies, "That is how God looks at you. No matter what has happened to you, no matter how tarnished you are, how crumpled, how many problems you have, you still have the same value to God." In this exercise people are given an object image to realize they have value regardless of their circumstances.

Tell a Story You Have Never Told Anyone

In this technique one group member pairs up with another member and tells a story about his or her life that he or she has never before told anyone. The story does not have to be embarrassing or private, just a story. This helps to develop listening and verbal skills.

The Sun Shines Down

This therapeutic activity is much like musical chairs. Chairs are positioned in a circle with one less chair than the number of people, so one person is left standing. The person standing says to the group, "The sun shines down on everyone who has been in an auto accident." Everyone who admits to having been in an accident will switch chairs, and the standing person goes for a chair too. Because there aren't enough chairs, it always leaves one person standing. That person then must say, "The sun shines down . . ." and offer an experience. One rule is that when you get up from a chair and can't find another, you cannot return to that same chair.

Some common comments include:

"The sun shines down on everyone who has . . .
Gotten drunk
Smoked pot
Stolen something

While this is a fun and popular ice breaker, it also serves to have group members confess guilt and shame in a way that is not threatening. Another benefit is that it helps the group leader to identify some of the issues that each person may be encountering.

CHAPTER 9

The Journey Continues

A drowning man does not complain about the size
of a life preserver.

—Anonymous

After one or more icebreaking techniques that have achieved alertness and unity in the group, the members are then prepared to engage in deeper therapeutic investigations. The purpose of these techniques is to enable all members to clearly focus on the group process while allowing each member to further explore individual struggles and personal issues. These processes are generally more therapeutic than the icebreaking processes.

Discovery Walk

The discovery walk is a technique that literally "walks" the participants from one therapeutic issue to another, helping to resolve a series of problems along the journey. This becomes especially effective for persons recovering from addictions, although it works well with all populations. The group leader prepares sheets with a word written on each one. Suggested categories that are written, one per paper, include:

Self
Addiction
Recovery
Mother

Father
Grandmother
Grandfather
Loved one
Child
Abuser
Illness
The deceased
God

Group members can also suggest other topics, such as the name of a brother or sister or friend to relate to individually. The papers are placed on the floor either in a line or around the room. One at a time, each member steps up to one card and talks to it. The person goes all the way down the line of selected cards, confronts the pertinent issues in his or her life, and is permitted to skip some if they are not relevant.

Another way to conduct this group is to put the papers randomly on the floor, dim the lights, and have participants look at all papers and decide which single topic they may want to confront during this session. The group leader should suggest that each member confront at least one relevant issue.

If the first card is *self*, then the person is encouraged to do a self-confrontation. A self-confrontation involves a participant stepping up to the card and pretending he is addressing himself. For example, John might say, "John, I am angry at you because you are so manipulative all the time. The other day, you alienated your girlfriend because you lied about smoking a joint. You swore you didn't, but she knew it. You should have been honest when she questioned you. You're busted, John." The group leader can step in and encourage John to continue to face other instances of manipulation and/or other personal problems he is denying.

Another way to do a self-confrontation is for John to pick another male in the group who is similar to him or knows him well enough to role-play him. The role player might then confront John with several observations regarding unhealthy habits and practices.

After self-confrontation, John may move on, or another participant may step up to a card. For example, Gloria may step up to the card labeled Father. She may point to a male group member and ask him to play her father. This member is coached not to react but to permit Gloria to discover her feelings. She may confront him about the sexual abuse she suffered as a preteen. The abusive role-playing father will confess that he is guilty and permit Gloria to release feelings of anger and hurt without reacting. After Gloria has expressed her feelings, the role-playing father is coached to beg for his daughter's forgiveness. The group leader will suggest to Gloria that she needs to eventually forgive her father because forgiving him even thought he doesn't deserve it will set her free.

A particularly touching part of the recovery is Mother. Most participants have deep pain about their mothers. For example, Susan may say, "I am sorry that I used drugs, Mother. I also stole your wedding ring and sold it for drugs. Please forgive me." These discoveries lead to helping the client gain more control and create a closer relationship with her mother.

In this fashion, members will confront one or more issues by stepping up to a sheet and, with or without using another member to help by role-playing, will release feelings and discover issues that hinder their personal growth.

Hot Seat

In this exercise, one member is asked to sit in a chair in the middle of the group. The other members are asked to give affirmations or constructive criticism to the member. This helps the member understand how others view him or her. In this exercise, a person receives substantial feedback. However, caution the group members giving feedback to keep criticism constructive. Instead of saying, "You are lazy," say, "Do you think you need to work more on your work ethic?" Very often the person who is sitting in the hot seat is asked to respond to the comments that have been made. It is equally important feedback for the group to hear the person respond to various comments and criticisms that have been directed toward him or her.

Another powerful way of running this group is to have the person blindfolded and sitting in the middle of the group. The group leader has various members whisper criticisms or compliments to the group leader and the leader then "edits" the comments to be more constructive and less critical before telling them to the blindfolded one. The purpose for the mediator is to reword the group members' comments so they don't upset or antagonize the blindfolded one. This can be extremely helpful when group members need feedback to learn how they are affecting others.

Coin Exercise

The purpose of this exercise is to ascertain the relative social development of the individual members within the group. For this exercise, one member at a time is given three coins: a penny, a dime, and a quarter. The member must then go to another group member that she likes, give that person the penny, and explain why she likes her or why she benefits from her. Next, the person goes to another member she likes a little better and gives away the dime and explains why she likes him or why she benefits from him. Finally, she gives away the quarter and explains the same. The group leader takes back the coins and has another member do the same, giving away the penny, the dime, and the quarter. Obviously, some members will be given coins more often than others. The members of the group should be encouraged to discuss why they received the coins from the others. For the members that were given the most quarters, the group can figure out what it is about them that caused that response. Also, the people who were given no coins or very few coins are encouraged to figure out why they did not receive coins. Maybe they need to work on certain social skills to be more liked or to become more influential among other group members.

Wounded Child

One technique developed by John Bradshaw requires one member in the middle of the group to be holding a teddy bear. This person is the wounded child. One by one, each group member approaches the child with the teddy bear, touches her on the shoulder, and says things that every little child needs to hear from a parent. The surrogate mothers and fathers might declare, "I love you," "you are beautiful," "I will protect you," or "I am glad you are a girl (or a boy)." Soft music is played in the background. Both surrogate parents and wounded child are affected by these gentle words.

Psychodrama

Psychodrama, the work of J. L. Marino, allows members to act out their life, their wishes, and their dreams on a stage with the group leader as director. There are a variety of psychodramas that can be performed including role-play, family sculpture, role reversal, the double technique, and the empty chair.

A. ROLE PLAY

Role-play is frequently utilized. Instead of describing what someone has done in the past, in role-play, the action is current and present. Instead of saying, "My dad abused me when I was a child," a scene is arranged and enacted in which the child addresses the abusive father. Often, the group member who is the abused child needs help to express the feelings in the here and now. The use of an alter ego is employed. This is another person, sometimes the therapist, who stands behind the abused child and feeds him the words he needs to say to the father. Similarly, the alter ego can stand behind the abusive father and supply his dialogue.

B. FAMILY SCULPTURE

One participant is selected to enact his family dynamics. As director of this psychodrama, he selects various group members to play a particular member of his family. He puts the person in a stereotyped posture, just like a statue. This actor is then required to remain in that position, neither moving nor speaking. The director completes the stage with his different family members in a variety of different positions and activities. For instance, he recalls his father reading the paper, his mother cooking dinner, and his little brother playing a computer game. Once in position, the director moves from statue to statue, from the person he has the least feelings about to the person with whom he has the most issues. He tells each statue what he is feeling about them. The statues remain mute and unresponsive. This allows the group member to express his negative and positive feelings toward family in a safe, protected environment.

For instance, one young man addressed his father who was reading the paper saying, "Father, I never knew you. You were always too busy for me. Even when you were around, you treated me as someone insignificant. I wish it were different. I find it difficult to relate to you now. I think of your neglect, and now I want to ignore you."

C. ROLE REVERSAL

In this technique, the person role-plays a significant person her life, e.g., the father, while another member of the group plays him or her. This offers the person a chance to stand in his or her father's shoes to help understand why his or her father said and did the things that he did. Often this can lead to a catharsis and eventually help the person achieve forgiveness and to move forward with the rest of his or her life.

D. THE DOUBLE TECHNIQUE

One member will ask another member of the group to play one of the conflicting aspects of his personality. For example, an ex-addict might choose a person to play his addiction while he role-plays his desire to be drug-free. The two characters must then debate the benefits of and reasons for each behavior and each point of view. The member then will alternate and play the addict who wants to be drug-free and his mate will play his addictive side.

Everyone has what is known as "top dog" and "underdog" aspects to his or her personality. The top dog is the conscience—the "thou shalts," the "you should get up in the morning," the "you should go to work," the "you should clean your house." The underdog is the part of the personality that does not want to work or do anything, wants to relax, and feels overstressed. A person may use the double technique to play these two sides—top dog and underdog—to better understand and better control these personality facets.

E. EMPTY CHAIR TECHNIQUE

In this process, the member imagines someone she is familiar with is sitting in an empty chair in the middle of the circle. She expresses her feelings to this imaginary person. The person might express to her mother that she loves her and is sorry she hurt her. The opposite feelings may also be expressed. A person may have feelings about a father who was abusive. He then uses this cathartic opportunity to address his father.

The same empty-chair technique can apply to the abovementioned "top dog and underdog." The top dog might say to the underdog, "You are evil, you are bad, you don't deserve to live. Why don't you go and kill yourself and get it over with?" The member would then sit in the empty chair and say as an underdog, "I just can't help all the bad things I do. I have no control over them, and anyway, I hate you for reminding me of them constantly." As the person begins to verbalize the real issues and feelings, he or she often becomes increasingly aware of her humanness and gains greater control of her individual behaviors. A person can take any polar conflict within the personality—good boy versus bad boy, passive self versus aggressive self—and likewise carry on a dialogue between the two.

F. THERAPEUTIC THEATER

Therapeutic Theater is similar to the discovery walk except it is a psychodrama with two chairs in the middle of the floor facing each other. The same discovery walk cards can be used and scattered on the floor, or new ones may be constructed. Again, common issues include: mother, father, child, self, addiction, or God. Have different members pick up a card and put the card on the opposite chair. Members then choose someone from the circle to role-play the person or issue written on that card. The member "confronts" that person or issue while soft music is playing in the background.

Gestalt: Dream Work or Fantasy Work

The gestalt therapist Fritz Pearls developed cathartic ways of helping people express their feelings from interpreting their dreams. Gestalt therapists teach clients to act out in the present tense and experience their dreams and fantasies rather than to interpret them as psychoanalysts teach. In gestalt therapy, the client presents a dream and then in psychodrama fashion acts out each element of that dream in the *now* (i.e. present tense) so that the client fully experiences each facet of the dream. Pearls explains that every dream symbol is a facet of the personality that needs to be expressed. A dream symbol can be anything in a dream: from a body part, a child's swing, or another person. Any element in a dream is part of the person's personality. Gestalt dream work makes for lively sessions that allow people to identify feelings.

One client in therapy had a dream of a witch chasing him down the street.

> Therapist: "Now you be yourself and tell me what you experienced."
>
> Client: "I am walking down the street and a horrible-looking witch is running after me laughing. I am trying to get away, but I can't run very fast. I just can't seem to get away from her. She is getting closer and closer."
>
> Therapist: "Very good. Now you be the witch."
>
> Client: "I am the witch. I am running after Joe because I don't like him. I am going to eat him up because he is more to me as meat than he is getting all the attention away from me alive. I don't like Joe."

In the case of Joe, Joe had a long history of self-destructive behaviors, with the female part of his personality trying to destroy him. After he came to the realization of his self-destructive side, (the witch), and integrated it into his personality, he gained better control of himself.

Self-Analysis Questions

Before the group, members are given questions to discuss. Participants may be asked to write down the answers at the beginning of the group therapy for discussion with the group at large later. One could even run an entire group session focusing on only one question. Other questions can be added to this list.

Sample questions to be used for self-analysis inventory:

1. How do you see yourself and your identity?
2. What do you think is your strongest asset?
3. What do you think is your weakest point?
4. What do you admire most in others?
5. What do you dislike most in others?
6. What was your mother's main criticism of you?
7. About what did your mother most compliment you?
8. What was your father's main criticism of you?
9. About what did your father most compliment you?

10. Other than your parents, who had the greatest influence on you and why?
11. How did you view yourself as a child?
12. What do you want most out of life?
13. What is your biggest fear in life?
14. If you could change something in you, what would it be?
15. What is your most common criticism of others?
16. When you were small, what advice do you remember most?
17. When you were small, how did you view the world?
18. Identify a traumatic experience in your life. How did you feel?

Art Therapy

There are many things one can do with a pencil and paper. Each member can draw a picture of their family and show it to the group. They can then talk about each person to the group. Another suggestion is to ask each member to draw a life line that symbolizes their life and the milestones in their life. The members can then talk to the group about the significant times of their life and how they felt about each of these developmental milestones.

You can make a clay figure of yourself and place it on the table with the figures made by other group members. Each group member can decide why he made the clay that particular shape or why she placed it where she did. There are available books on art therapy that offer many useful details and suggestions.

Talk To A Picture

For a grieving group, this process is invaluable. Members are asked to bring in a photograph of a significant loved one. Each client is encouraged to talk to that picture. Since many individuals are grieving over lost ones but have never adequately released these hurt feelings, looking at the photograph enables them to more easily remember that person and release all the unspoken emotions toward the loved one. Clients greatly benefit by getting feelings out that they would never have normally been able to express.

Judy was unstable and suicidal after the death of her mother.
"Judy, how are you feeling?" asks the leader.

"I can't take the pain. It feels so bad. I want to stop it. I want to hurt myself so bad."

"Did you bring your mother's picture?" the leader inquires.

"I did," Judy replies, reaching into her purse.

"Now hold her picture up and look at it carefully and remember."

"I can't! I can't! It makes me feel worse," Judy says, turning her head away.

"Do it anyway. You need to experience the pain before you can feel better. Say,

'Mommy, you know how I feel about you.'"

"Mommy, do you know how I feel about you?" Judy asks glancing at the photo and then looking away.

"Tell her," she is coached.

"I love you. I miss you. I have no one left. I am alone. I am lonely." Judy starts to cry as a group member offers her a tissue.

"Keep going, Judy. You are doing well. Say what you are feeling."

"I can't do this!" Judy looks at the group.

"Yes, you can. Tell your mother how she died."

"You died in the fire. I couldn't get to you. The smoke was too thick. I couldn't save you. I'm sorry, Mommy."

Women on either side of Judy touch her shoulders in support.

"I'm sorry, Mommy. I feel so responsible. I couldn't save you," Judy sobs deeply.

'Keep saying it," coaches the facilitator. "Come on. Get it out. Get it all out."

Judy continues to wail loudly about how she couldn't save her mother. Later the group facilitator says, "Tell Mom about the bad times. Tell her how helpless she felt about watching your father drink himself to death and refuse help."

After Judy relates the bad times, the facilitator then encourages her. "Tell Mom about the good times."

Tears of sadness turn to tears of joy as Judy told Mom about her high school graduation with relatives bringing presents for her and her grandparents beaming with pride for their granddaughter.

A Problem Group

Each group member is given a paper and pencil and told to write down a serious problem that keeps reoccurring and needs to be healed. It could be a health issue, a drug addiction, an interpersonal relationship, an eating disorder, or a smoking problem. The group members are then asked to write responses to the following concerning their individually identified problem:

1. The theme or the problem that reoccurs
2. The first memory of the problem
3. Feelings that the problem evokes
4. The body sensation that the problem evokes and where it is felt in the body
5. The advantage or good feeling gained from the problem (secondary gain)
6. The price or consequence paid for this problem
7. What can be done to overcome this problem

The goal is to help members identify and analyze these therapeutic problems. Then they are asked to discuss them with the larger group. Often the group gives significant feedback to various problems.

Confession Booth

While the group is running, one of the mental health workers can ask for any volunteers who would like to go to the confession booth. That is simply an area apart from the group where they can confess under complete confidentiality, just like the Catholic confession booth. The person can talk about any shame and guilt that may be occurring and needs to be gotten off their chest. When people avail themselves of the confession booth, they report great relief through becoming totally and completely honest in the privacy of only one listening therapist.

Prepared Letter Process

"Sorrow looks back. Worry looks around. Faith looks up." A prepared letter (e.g., from the devil or God or a deceased person) can be read to the group to encourage people to talk about feelings. Always, appropriate music is played in the background. Sample letters that could be read for a particular group follow:

A Letter from Your Addiction

I have come to visit you once again. I love to see you suffer mentally, physically, spiritually, and socially. I want to make you restless so you can never relax. I want you to be jumpy and nervous and anxious. I want to make you agitated, irritable, and depressed so that you cannot think clearly or positively. I want to make you hate everything and everybody, especially yourself. I want to make you feel guilty and remorseful for the things you have done in the past that you will never be able to let go of. I want to make you angry and hateful toward the world for the way it is and the way you are. I want to make you fearful and paranoid for no reason at all. I want to wake you at all hours of the night screaming for me. You know you cannot sleep without me. Even in your dreams you think about me. I want to be the first thing you wake up to every morning and the last thing you touch before you black out. I would rather kill you, but I will be happy to put you in the hospital or an institution or jail. But you know I'll still be waiting for you when you get out. I love to watch you going slowly insane. I love to see all the physical damage that I am causing you. I can't help but sneer and chuckle when you shiver and shake, when you freeze and sweat at the same time that you wake with your blanket soaking wet. It is amazing to watch you make love to the toilet bowl, heaving and retching and not being able to hold me down. It is amazing how much destruction I can do to your internal organs while at the same time destroying your brain bit by bit. I deeply appreciate how much you sacrifice for me, the countless jobs you have sacrificed for me, and all the fine friends you deeply cared for and abandoned for me. What's more, the ones you turned against yourself because of your inexcusable actions, I am even more grateful for, and especially your loved ones, your family, and the most important people in the world to you. You even threw them away for me. I cannot express in words the gratitude I have for the loyalty you have for me. You sacrificed all those beautiful things in life just to devote yourself completely to me. But after you have lost all these things, you can still depend on me to take even more. You can depend on me to keep you in a living hell and to keep your mind, body, and soul as mine. I will not be satisfied until you are dead, my friend.

Sincerely,
Your Addiction,
Author Unknown

Another letter that can be used in a Christian audience is a love letter from Jesus.

A Letter from Jesus

How are you? I just had to send you this letter to tell you how much I care about you and love you. I saw you yesterday as you were walking with your friends. I waited all day long hoping you would walk and talk with me too. As evening drew near, I gave you a sunset to close your day and a cool breeze to soothe your cheek. Did you like it? And I waited, but you never came. Oh, yes, it hurt me, but I still love you because I am your friend. I saw you fall asleep last night. I longed to touch your brow, so I spilled moonlight on your pillow and on your face. Did you feel it? Again, I waited, wanting to rush down so we could talk. I have so many gifts for you. You awakened late this morning and rushed into the day. My tears were in the rain. Today you looked so sad and alone. It makes my heart ache because I understand. My friends let me down and hurt me many times. But I love you. I tried to tell you in the quiet green grass. I whisper in the leaves and in the trees. I breathe it in the color of the flowers. I shout to you in the mountain streams and give the bird love songs to sing just to you. I clothe you in warm sunshine and perfume the air. My love for you is deeper than the oceans and bigger than the largest want or need you could have ever. We will spend eternity together in heaven. I know how hard it is on earth. I really do know because I was there. I want to help you. My father wants to help you too. He is that way, you know. Let me ask you this question. Let's say you had a child who did all the bad things that you did and even worse. Would you still love that child? Of course you would. That's the way I feel about you. Just call me. Talk to me. I'm waiting; it's your decision. I have chosen you, and because of this, I will wait. Yes, I am waiting because I love you and you are my friend. You are so important you are even worth dying for.

Your Friend,
Jesus
Author Unknown

Dream Table

The average person has about five dreams a night. Each group member is encouraged to tell the group of a dream that has occurred. After the telling, use volunteers or pick several (about four) group members each in turn say, "If that were my dream, I believe it would mean" And the members tell what it would mean to them. Importantly, in the group, nobody acts as the dream expert; each volunteer just shares what they think the dream would mean to them.

After the volunteers have shared, the leader would then ask the dreamer if he got any insights into the dream. Very often, many incredible insights are shared by the dreamer. Often people that may be sharing a dream are also sharing a real-life experience that they have had but are disguising it as a dream. This covert confession of a traumatic experience is very freeing for a person who has hidden an incident for years.

CHAPTER 10

Guided Imagery

*When you're successful you don't appreciate all the magic
that went into that success as much as when you've gone through
failure when you try something and it doesn't work, you have a
tendency to spend time reflecting.*

—Jason Rasky

When sensitivity groups are offered to the community at large, an atmosphere prevails with the focus on making the participants feel comfortable. Group attendants are encouraged to bring a blanket and/or pillow and a teddy bear for comfort because participants often have to sit on the floor. After initial relaxation and/or icebreakers, group members are encouraged to sit on their blankets on the floor, often hugging their teddy bears. The lights are dimmed, and the room temperature is comfortable. Background instrumental music is played to create a mood that encourages honesty and openness. A candle is lit in the middle of groups of eight to twelve people. Often lollipops or hard candy pieces may be provided. The goal is to make members as relaxed as possible.

To choose the small group members from the total attendees, several methods may be employed. Whichever way is used, each group must have at least one trained leader. Additionally, no one must know anyone else previously, that is, friends or relatives should not be in the same group. Anonymity is stressed whenever possible.

Sensitivity groups are partially based on guided imagery. Guided imagery is a personal exploration of inner space. A group leader initiates imaginary pictures to relax, to evoke, to plan, or to examine past or future scenarios. The individual is encouraged through dialogue to interact with these images based on one's own needs and experiences.

One image that is often evoked is a *safe place*. When techniques have been employed to successfully calm and relax the group attendees, the group facilitator, through music and words, guides the participants back in time to a safe place from their past experiences (e.g., on the beach or in their bedroom). Once this safe place is successfully established, a person can retreat to this imaginary safe haven to relax if anxiety or distress occurs.

The most commonly used guided imagery technique for our sensitivity groups is the photo album process. Members are asked to imagine that they are leafing through the pages of a photo album, seeing familiar people and faces and allowing the feelings associated with each of these images to surface. They may view persons they loved but who rejected them; they may view someone who abused them or someone who provided security and comfort for them. Members may also be asked to view themselves at certain developmental stages. Some images invoked include that of a mother, father, deceased, infant, birthday, funeral, graveyard, illness, death, childhood, worst experience, or best experience.

As each image is introduced, the group facilitator narrates through background music. This dialogue encourages the members to recreate their relationship with the person or situation. Feelings invoked are often shouted. Participants are encouraged to scream, "I hate you. You hurt me" or "I love you. I miss you."

While everyone may be doing this at the same time, with two hundred people in one room, a great amount of anonymity occurs. Because each person is paying attention to his own issue and not listening to others, privacy does occur. While this may appear chaotic and unsupervised, with proper music and imagery, emotions are healed. Before the group ends, each person is encouraged to have talked to a variety of images while hugging the pillow or teddy bear for comfort.

As each image is presented and processed, the narrator might say, "Turn to the next page of your photo album and you will see the picture of a man. This man is your father." At this point, a song about a father will be played and words to the song will be spoken to help evoke feelings about the father. The narration continues. "Did you love him? Did you hate him? Did he hurt you? Did you hurt him? Just look at your father's face and feel the feelings in your body. Think about what you need to say to your father. Did you love your father? If so, let me hear you say so over and over. Yell it out. Say 'I love you, Daddy.' Anybody here hate your father? Just look at this photo album and say 'I hate you, Daddy.' Say it louder. Shout it out. Say, I hate you. Now, everybody, no matter what feeling you are feeling, yell out that feeling toward your father. Say, 'Daddy I feel . . .' and yell the feeling louder." The narrator pauses and begins again. "Now tell Daddy why you feel the way you do. Everybody, make some noise. If you can't think about a feeling, just scream. Tell your father what you feel, get it out now. It will make you feel better. It will help you heal a broken heart."

Sometimes we will actually have a person with a fatherly voice role-play Father and say things like, "Do you love me? Do you hate me? Yell it out. I can't hear you. I am sorry. I could have been a better father. Will you please forgive me? I can't hear you."

Sometimes we may use a female's maternal voice to play Mother and say, "Hi, child, I'm here. Tell me what you feel about me. I can't hear you. Louder. Did you love me? Tell me you love me. Did you hate me? Tell me you hate me. Tell me whatever you feel. I am only going to be here for a few minutes, so tell me what you feel inside. I can't hear you. Say it louder. Say it louder. Was I a good mother? Was I a bad mother?"

The photo album image may also feature a child. Individuals must decide who the child is. It could be themselves or one of their own children. Background music featuring a child's voice will be used. Members are encouraged to talk to this child.

There are variations instead of using a photo album. Sometimes the members imagine being given a shoebox, and they remove pictures out of this shoebox one at a time. Sometimes they are given an imaginary wallet with photographs in it. Members are encouraged to bring actual pictures of their mother or father or family members and talk to these real photographs.

Another variation of this process has the person imagining being in a long hall and walking up to a closed door, opening the door, and entering into a traumatic incident from his or her past life. The member will examine this event and respond to it similarly to the photo album by saying and shouting the emotions. Then the member journeys down the hall to open another door where mother could be sitting in a chair.

The member talks to mother and then continues to open doors into life's various rooms as a way of enabling members to review people and places that evoke therapeutic issues.

A person might turn to a photo of himself or herself. In a particularly disorderly life, the person might confront himself, yell at himself, and release feelings of guilt and shame in this type of imaginary role-playing.

Another variation is to incorporate the letter writing process. Give each group member a sheet of paper with a label on top. One label may say Mother, Father, Abuser, or Deceased. Members will actually write a letter to their mother, their father, abuser, or deceased. One by one they will read their letter to the group. All father letters will be read, then the mother letters, etc. As participants are reading these letters, appropriate thematic background music is being played.

Another photo album imagery turns the participants toward their future. Is there marriage in their future? Are there children in their future? Are they happy? Do they make healthy decisions? Do they continue to make many mistakes in their lives?

The narrator can also bring up different times of the year. People can imagine Christmas trees at Christmas time and identify who is around the tree and who is missing from the scene. (People who do not celebrate this holiday can also relate.) Another scenario that works well is to have clients imagine a current or future birthday and identify who is present or absent for this celebration.

Vary the imagery activity by distributing a 3x5 card to each member. They are asked to fill both sides of the card with secrets that they are afraid to tell anyone. Leaders assure participants that no one will read the cards and encourage them to be honest. Inform the group that what has been written on these cards can be erased for good. At the end of this group activity, participants are asked to hold the cards up to God and ask God to forgive them for the things they have done and for their guilt and shame. The imagery concludes with having their cards torn up, a symbolic way of showing that they have been forgiven.

Another 3x5 card exercise also calls on God and prayer. On one side of the card, participants write what they are thankful for from God, and on the other side, they write a prayer request or what they want from God. At the end of the group, members exchange these prayer cards with someone else in the group. They take these cards home and pray for that other person and his or her requests. This reinforces the power of prayer and helps members remember the group.

Another approach requests the members to visualize an imaginary balloon and to write on the balloon their feelings toward someone who is deceased. People might write, "I love you. I miss you." They imagine releasing that helium balloon up into the sky. The narrator instructs the group to pretend that the balloon is floating toward the person who is deceased. The deceased person, played by the narrator, then says, "I see you down there. I am sitting up here on this cloud, and the balloon is coming toward me. Let me see if I can touch it. There, I have it . . . Yes, I have the balloon. I see on this balloon that you say that you love me and that you miss me and that you cried over me. I want you to know that I love you too and that I miss you very much. I am proud that you are moving on with your life and doing the best you can. I am looking forward to seeing you, and I care about you very much. I have talked to God, and He said He is going to send a guardian angel to watch over you. Don't be in any hurry to come up and see me. God has a purpose for you. Fulfill that purpose. Live a long wonderful life."

A technique called the "number one/number two" process can be used with teenagers that are reluctant to participate in other guided imageries. Using the same themes such as mother, father, abuser, or deceased, participants are put in pairs. They hold hands, and number one talks first to number two. Number One closes his eyes and imagines he is holding the hands of his mother. He vocalizes his previously unspoken feelings toward his mother. Number Two is usually silent but can encourage number one to get his or her feelings out. In the background, thematic motherly music is played. After Number One has finished and has talked to his mother for five to ten minutes, then Number Two will close his eyes and talk to Number One as his imagery mother. Number Two will imagine that Number One's hands are the hands of his mother.

Some resistant teenagers do not want to keep their eyes closed and may look at each other and laugh. To help eliminate this problem, this "kneel at the chair" process uses guided imagery. Have them kneel (using pillows under their knees) with their elbows into a chair and with their backs to the group. That way, the young people are not looking into each other's faces and can instead focus on talking to the photograph of their mother, father, or abuser without having any fear that someone else is looking at their faces.

Chapter 11

A Secrets Group

You are only as sick as your secrets.

—SEW

"Falling down doesn't make you a failure, but staying down does." The objective of a secrets group is to help a person reduce anxiety by anonymously revealing one's deepest secrets in a setting where people are accepting and nonjudgmental. Many people have secrets that are deeply hidden from others and even from themselves. Secrets groups are used to heal by helping participants discuss secrets out in a safe, confidential atmosphere. By creating an accepting atmosphere, a person can hear someone else role-play his or her secret. A secrets group is a real trust and confidence builder and generally contributes to a participant's self-esteem because through revealing the shame and guilt of the hidden secret, one is often released from this secret.

Preparing The Group

Fundamental rules should apply. The leader chooses the group members with optimal groups between seven and twelve people. Members of the group should be strangers to each other. When two people know one another, embarrassing or unpleasant family secrets may be revealed. Sometimes you can run a group with just females, or sometimes a secrets group can run with just males. Sometimes, secrets groups are done on the floor; sometimes there is a chair group. Groups can be done in a different language. For instance, someone might conduct a group entirely in Spanish for those who are not fluent in English.

Stress confidentiality. Carefully reinforce that whatever is said in the group stays in the group and is not to be repeated outside the group. If a person speaks outside the group about a shared secret, others will confront him or her. This explanation is vital for if a person hears a secret repeated outside the group, trust will be greatly reduced, and future group discussions become more difficult to conduct because of distrust. Many participants come to group already extremely distrusting and all care needs to be taken to build trust. Secondly, the members are told that they are not to judge or laugh at a person's secret. They are forbidden from saying things such as, "I would never do such a thing or such a thing never happened to me." Also group participants are assured that the card on which they write will be destroyed after their secret is presented. The group leader assures that all cards are torn into pieces and disposed of and that no one keeps a secret card.

Basic materials the group leader needs to include are pencils, 3x5 index cards, tissues, a large empty cup for disposing of torn-up index cards, and a flashlight because the room should have lights dimmed. All participants use the same color pencils, no pens, so as to assume anonymity of secrets written on the index card. A secrets group usually runs one to two hours in duration.

The Group

> *Was it the wounded places down inside people that*
> *sought each other out,*
> *that bred a kind of love between them?*
> —Sue Monk Kidd

The leader distributes the index cards and asks the members to write their worst secret on it. This secret is to be one that they have never told anyone or one that has bothered them severely. Sometimes, the leader might ask the members to write more than one secret on more than one card. A blank card in the pack may mean that a member cannot read. The leader should also privately offer to write a member's secret for them if one does not write and later read it if the person does not read. Occasionally, with certain populations, participants will not write deep secrets. When this occurs, the group leader may collect all the written secrets, tear them up, and tell the group to get serious. Remind participants that they are only as sick as their secrets and will not get any benefit from the group if they are not honest.

After all secrets are discussed, the group members are given an opportunity to give feedback on the group. If someone wants to reveal that a particular secret is his, he may. However, members are not permitted to guess whose secret belongs to whom. In some cases, if a person has a serious secret, other group participants may urge the person to get counseling for that problem.

As healing and trust develop, deeper and deeper issues are revealed. While some group members may not be very honest, others are surprisingly honest. As trust builds in the group, people start admitting to their secrets and discussing them openly. When a group meets every week or biweekly, a secrets group can occur as often as once a month.

Secrets we have heard revealed include:

- I have had several abortions.
- I ran over a child with my car and left the scene of the accident.
- I was raped.
- I killed my cousin.
- I am afraid I am a homosexual.
- I cannot read.

Once the secret is written, the group leader collects all the cards and shuffles them carefully. The cards are then redistributed, one to each member. Either the members may pick one from the stack with the writing facing downward or the leader may hand one to each person. In either case, the leader tells the members that if they get their own card back, which is possible, they are to pretend it still is someone else's secret. Each group member silently reads the secret on the card they have received. Then each person reads the secret on the card aloud. The group can then begin discussing the most serious secrets first. For example, a sexual abuse secret would precede a secret regarding stealing money. However, all secrets must be discussed as it is important not to belittle anyone's secret. When several secrets are similar, these secrets can be presented together.

The group is now ready to discuss the first secret. The leader selects a card and has the member reread it and pretend that he or she is the one with that secret. Even if the secret is "I have had five abortions" and the reader is male, he pretends he is that female and tries to put himself behind that woman's eyes when responding to that secret and the feelings pertaining to it.

Without judging, the other members of the group are then to give advice and support to this "role-player." If participants are reticent to offer support, the group leader must facilitate it by giving helpful advice and encouragement to the holder of the secret. Again, emphasize that no member is to judge that secret. After each secret is discussed, the card is torn up and discarded.

Finally, the members can end the group with a prayer (perhaps the Serenity Prayer) or a slogan. Before dispersing, have each group member affirm or give some form of encouragement to each other member. Hugs and positive comments are encouraged.

CHAPTER 12

The Journey Pauses

Life can only be understood by looking backward,
but it must be lived by looking forward.

—Unknown

Feedback

At the end of the group session, each member is asked for feedback. Feedback is essential for group leaders to know how the participants have benefited and so they can use this feedback to adjust future group sessions to better fulfill the members' needs. What was most helpful or least helpful? This question gives the leaders specific information for constructing future groups.

It is advisable to pass out anonymous evaluation sheets to allow members to honestly state on paper what they might not say to the group or its leader. A group leader may ask if there was anything that was said in the group that offended anyone. Sometimes people will divulge information or other private thoughts through this anonymous honest feedback opportunity. Leaders must be open to feedback and change so their techniques do not stagnate.

What Are You Going To Do?

The most important question to ask at the end of a therapy group or at the end of an individual session is "Now, what are you going to do?" The member focuses on the future, which often gives a person hope. Each person is asked to think about a plan of action that can be helpful. Carl Jung said that every therapist should have clients discuss their future and future plans toward the end of a session because obviously a person who is depressed is caught up in the past, and help a person get over depression, a positive plan of action is needed. Carl Jung concludes that it is never helpful to leave a session where the person just discusses the past and then require him or her to come back next week.

Slogan or Song or Prayer

"God intervenes in the affairs of men by invitation only." A group may conclude with a saying or an inspiring poem or a song. Sometimes a group member with a good singing voice can perform. Often the group may have a theme song to be sung together for motivation and solidarity. In groups with alcoholics and drug addicts, the Serenity Prayer is often cited. Prayer as an ending also allows everyone to tell God what they are thankful for or to ask God for what they still need for healing. Often the Lord's Prayer is an effective ending. Documented by Dorsey in *Prayer is Good Medicine* (1996), prayer does work and even sometimes heals. Despite the current era of political correctness, one does not eliminate what has worked for generations. People should never allow adversity to get them down—except on their knees. "To anyone of you in trouble, he should pray" (James 5:13).

"With These Hands I Will"

"Sometimes we are so busy adding up our troubles that we forget to count our blessings." Everyone in the group says, "With these hands, I will." Members repeat that phrase a few times, and then the leader starts, "With these hands, I will." The leader then states what he or she is going to do with these hands in the future to make life and the world a better place to live. The next person then says, "With these hands I will," and finishes the sentence. Everyone in the group makes an affirmation, helping people to focus positively on the future.

Hug Other Members with Feedback

"The heart is the happiest when it beats for others." In the proper setting, group members can be asked to hug other group members and to affirm and to encourage them with "I love you" or "Good job today."

Dance

Group members often like to end the group with a dance. Doing the gospel slide or the cha-cha or the twist or some popular song leaves participants motivated and upbeat after the weighty issues and difficult processings of the group. It is beneficial to dismiss the group with positive, invigorating memories.

Affirmations

Many groups end with a go-round of personal affirmations: "I am a child of God," "I am somebody," "I love myself," and many others gleaned from *One Day at a Time* or any meditation guidebook.

CHAPTER 13

Music and Dance Therapy

Music is your own experience, your thoughts, your wisdom.
If you don't live it, it won't come out your horn.
—Charlie Parker

Many people do not easily feel comfortable dancing. When first taught nontechnical, simple group dances, people can begin to come out of their shells. Dance builds confidence. Since music and dance involve the kinesthetic and nonverbal parts of our being, this venue can help people to feel better about themselves and to be more open when it is time to share innermost feelings. In prison programs, homeless programs, or even with individuals who may be somewhat lethargic and unenthusiastic, just getting people up and moving their arms and legs to music or singing songs is beneficial in tearing down walls and allowing group leaders to communicate better with the participants. Even depressed people, when they cooperate, tend to respond well to music and dance, and sometimes, this helps more rapidly to lift their depressions. Even though the optimum group may range from six to twelve people, the reality is that many counselors deal with larger group numbers. Therefore, dance and music becomes a tool you can utilize with any number or population of people.

When using music and dance therapy, it is often a good idea to start out with people who are interested in cooperating and build the numbers as other people are included. One can start sessions with music and dance for just those who want to participate and then announce that for the next group, all others will be invited to join. In a residential facility, very often that is what happens. Once people watch the others enjoy dancing, more reluctant members get drawn into participating. Or by use of group pressure and/or encouragement, some individuals get drawn in and anticipate the dance section of the next group.

If a group has males and females, naturally there is even more energy for dance and music. Females tend to like music and dance more than males, but males reap just as much benefit from the music when they cooperate. Important to using dance in a therapeutic setting is to teach group dance. Stress that participants are *not* to pair off into male-female pairs but to remain in a group. The activity is a unisex dance so as not to encourage lust issues to arise between males and females within the group.

When introducing dance into a group setting, start with the more simple ones, ones that take little instruction or straining, such as marches or the paintbrush dance. Then the dances can get more complicated as the program continues. The most important instruction to give is "The only requirement when you dance is to know that it is okay to make many mistakes."

Note must be taken as to the ethnicity of the participants. With an ethnic mixture, a mixture of song venues is appropriate. Depending on the mood one wants to create through music and song, select the music that works best. Watch the various groups' responses to the music, and also note the evaluations completed by the participants at the end of the sessions.

The Feeling Dance or the Feeling Walk

The feeling dance helps people to be aware of the variety of feelings their body holds. The group leader selects songs and music to represent certain feelings to be evoked. Participants are asked to dance, walk, or enact the emotion identified by the leader and suggested by the music. One might ask that participants think about something that makes them angry. Use a fast song, or an angry song, with or without words, to bring up that feeling. Participants then dance or walk to that anger, depending on how they feel. Then the music and narrator can move to pain, and participants will act like they are in pain. Music should also be used to express joy, love, happiness, or fear. As participants become comfortable with this form of expression, members can suggest a feeling. The process can move to a person who expresses himself or herself by acting out the feeling that is being experienced. The facilitator does not need to intervene at this time.

Carnival Line or the Caterpillar March

In this activity the members put their left hand on the shoulder of the person in front of them and form a line. Carnival Lines should be no longer than ten to fifteen people. If there are more, divide members into two or more lines. Play some type of fast music and begin dancing around the room in your line. Participants may wave their free hand up in the air and when another line comes slap the other people with the free right hands. March around the room as the group leader weaves the line in arches, curves, or circles. Do not allow the lines to become bunched up in a big circle. Keep lines moving and weaving around the free space in the room and try to prevent the lines from becoming intertwined or bogging down. The carnival line is used to create excitement and uplifted spirits.

Dancing to Jazz

Jazz music allows movement without words. Group leaders can initiate warm-ups and stretching exercises and modern dance movements to jazz music for participants to imitate. It is not so much that correct movements are taught, but rather it is showing movements for people to attempt to mimic. The emphasis is not on a right or wrong technique; it is on just getting into the feeling of the music.

Have participants act out an image. For instance, play jazz music with few words and have participants pretend that they are a seed, all bunched up in a ball on the floor. Then the instructor might say that seed germinates and grows and protrudes upward through the soil, getting taller and taller, and she spread her arms out as the seed grows bigger. Participants are encouraged to imitate this movement. Then the wind comes and bends the tree in the wind. The birds sit on its branches. The temperature becomes very hot and then very cold, and the tree reacts to the various seasons. As fall comes, the leaves begin to dry. The plant gets old and starts to wither and goes back to the soil. People love acting out these images. This process helps them recognize and reflect on the cycles of life while being physically involved.

Another fun image is called "babysitting. Clients pretend they are babysitting and holding the baby. They play with the baby and hold it up in the air and laugh and roll around with the baby to jazz music. The narrator then tells them to notice the baby's diaper is dirty. Participants must smell it. They imitate the instructor as she holds her nose. Then the individuals put the baby on the floor, bathe the baby, and put on a fresh new diaper. The goal is to make the baby feel comfortable once more, and finally to music rock the baby to sleep.

A facilitator can think of several humorous situations that make people laugh or curl up their noses. Jazz or other kinds of music can facilitate the expression of these scenarios. Some can use words, but very often it is good to use music that does not have words.

Psychodrama to Music

1. Playground

The narrator starts, "You are eight years old and you live in an apartment. You are playing in the playground." The facilitator has some group members pretend they are eight-year-old children jumping rope, acting like they are playing double dutch, basketball, stick ball, and playing football. Members act out these types of activities to music. The narrator continues, "It is starting to get dark and your mother is calling out the windows for you to come in but you are having too much fun, so you continue to play. Then your mother comes out of the building and spanks you and grabs you by the scruff of the neck and pulls you back into the house as you go screaming and yelling and crying."

This psychodrama is designed to bring up fond, innocent memories. As the facilitator lets this scenario go, this dance can transition into the gang fight with more dramatic background music.

2. Gang Fight

People are instructed to freeze where they are and pretend that they are now sixteen years old. Divide the group into the Crips and the Bloods. Move the two groups to opposite sides of the room and suggest that they are going to have a rumble tonight. They are going to meet in the darkness of the playground. Have the Crips form a line and one end of the line walks in front of the Bloods, looking them in the face with a threatening manner using a song such as "Romeo Must Die." Then go back across the other side of the room and have the Bloods walk in front of the Crips, looking them in the face in a threatening manner. They walk in a line past the Crips and back to their side of the room. Then both sides walk toward each other in a menacing manner and they walk back. Next, two members dance in the middle of the floor, maybe two females, who will act like they are fighting although they will not hit each other. Then a male of the Crips and one of the Bloods come to the middle and they act like they are fighting and hitting each other until they back off. Then the two groups come toward each other and act like they are fighting in a rhythmic way. All of a sudden, shots ring out and everyone gets down. Participants find through pantomime that one of the group's members is dead and the people run. The drama then transitions into a funeral.

3.   Funeral

In this next scene the group witnesses a mock funeral. Music such as *Sorry I Never Told You* or *Gangster Lean* or *It's Hard to Say Goodbye to Yesterday* is played. Both the Crips and the Bloods show up at the funeral and walk around in a big circle as the role playing mother and the role playing father and maybe a role playing sibling are there mourning the dead person who is laying on the floor under a sheet with his head out and his arms folded. These family members yell at the Crips and the Bloods and tell them that the violence has to stop. The role playing mother looks at the group and yells, "You young punks. You killed my son. You killed my son! Stop the killing. Stop the killing!"

For people who have been involved in these types of behaviors, this psychodrama raises awareness to what they have been doing. They often become reflective and later on the clinician can use this enactment to help clients discuss how they felt and what they learned from this experience. For example, this psychodrama was performed in a youth facility with several clients who had been gang members. By transitioning from Playground to Gang fight to Funeral, this sequence of dances demonstrated for the teens how their lives had come from the innocent child to the thug gang member. The intense pain that swept over these teens as they realized the consequences of their "gang banging" was profound. Several graduates of these youth programs have confessed that these scenes became imbedded into their minds and served as one experience to aid in their healing process.

Soul Train

This is the traditional soul train, used in therapy groups to break the ice and offer everyone an opportunity to participate. However, don't line the females up on one side or the males up on the other side. Form two lines, with both males and females mixed as to avoid having males and females pair off. Encourage people to do group dances only. Soul train works well with the song "Follow Me."

Mirror Image or Mirror Dance

The mirror image or mirror dance can be used with any number of people from ten to hundreds. One person goes in the middle when the facilitator plays music. This person does very simple moves. He might scratch his head or wave his arms. Everyone else in the circle is encouraged to mirror what he or she is doing and move in a similar way. One does this for about a minute and then chooses someone else from the circle to come in the middle and do the same. That person does a move or a dance for a while and she picks another person and it goes on and on. In large groups of people, break the group up into circles of twenty and have the same music and each circle doing a mirror image within their particular group. This activity gets people involved because there is no standard movement required so no one feels inadequate. Also, members must remain alert for they can be chosen next to perform an action.

Line Dancing or Gospel Dancing

Line dancing or gospel dancing involves movements that are similar to those done by gospel choirs in which they clap their hands and wave their arms to certain phrases. One is "My Mind Is Made Up, No Turning Back," and when the song says, "My mind's made up," participants point to their heads. Then members can put their hands up and then circle their hands around in front of them. When the song says, "No turning back," instruct clients to point over their shoulders with their thumbs and clap their hands. Participants get in lines, and they clap their hands on either side of their body and move their shoulders. A group leader can also lead a march around the room and the group members will imitate the leader's movements. A popular song for this dance is "YMCA."

The Electric Slide and the Cha-cha Slide

With a group of individuals that are very enthusiastic about dancing and come together on a regular basis, teach them the electric slide and cha-cha slide. To start the dance, the leader gives a demonstration of the movements and encourages the members to try the movement without music first. Then when the music is played the leader again comforts the participants by reminding them that there are plenty of mistakes to be made and that they emphasis is on having fun. Interestingly enough, the electric slide works with various songs, some fast, some slow. Clients really enjoy this. Take other songs and have participants sing and dance to these. Again, do not encourage anyone to pair up with a person of the opposite sex.

Sing Songs

The more people, generally the more energy there is in the room. One idea is to have the males sit down and have the females stand up and sing a song to the males. Sometimes we use Deborah Cox, *How Did You Get Here*, or *I Will Survive*. After the females have sung and have taken their bow, the males get up and sing a song like *Mamma* by Boyz II Men, or *I'll Always Love My Momma*, or some other popular song. Sometimes the group leader needs to tell the group the words or give them word sheets if the group is not familiar with the songs. This is often motivating and fun for the people.

CHAPTER 14

The Genogram

Nothing has a stronger influence psychologically
on their environment and
especially on their children than the unlived life of the parent.
—Carl Jung

Family systems or systemic therapists examine the dynamics of the family. In one way or other, everyone belongs to a family and how we develop (psychodynamic), how we learn (behaviorism), how we think (cognitive), where we exist (existentialism) or what is our life story (humanism) all relate back to our Family of Origin. Significant to our healing and well being thus becomes an examination of one's family.

The major tool to enable this inspection is the genogram. As defined by Guerin and Pendagast (1976) a genogram is "a structural diagram of a family's three-generational relationship system." Monica McGoldrick (1999) with a few simple symbols; a square, a circle, some straight lines, and some wavy lines; creates a key that unlocks a veritable treasure trove of information about oneself and one's family. From this simple schematic the entire family story unfolds, allowing the person complete freedom to interpret the family saga.

For purposes of this exercise, the Identified Patient will be each individual group participant. Once he has created the genogram and has identified himself on it, everything else will fall into place.

The genogram has four parts:

- The schematic, the squares and circles

- The narrative, a description of what the schematic means
- The time-line schematic—what has happened in the client's life
- The time-line narrative, describing those major events in the client's life.

The basic symbols for a genogram are:

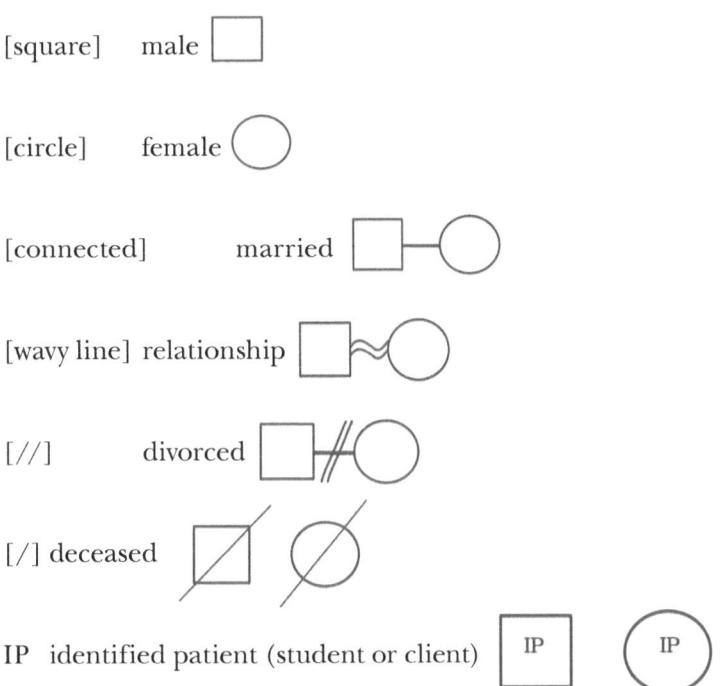

[square]   male

[circle]   female

[connected]   married

[wavy line] relationship

[//]   divorced

[/] deceased

IP   identified patient (student or client)   IP   IP

Family systems therapy does not focus on a patient, but believes that the system is at fault and one part of the system "acts out" to bring attention to the problem. Usually, the family wants to "fix" that acting out part. The parents may bring the student to the school psychologist and say "he's broke, fix him." The child is not broken, the system is in need of repair and the child is simply reporting it. The Systemic Therapist then considers that acting out family member as the "Identified Patient."

While the genogram may look like a family tree, which is a piece of it, it is not only considering who begat whom, but what the relationships are between the various members of the family. With the squares and circles all laid out, there begins to appear certain gaps. "Whatever happened to . . .? Who really was our great grandfather?" These questions allow people to research their own family to find the answers.

There is an anecdotal story about Murray Bowen, (Hoffman, L. 1981) which suggests he carefully went to all his family members to create his genogram. After collecting all the stories, he wrote each family member, to thank them and to inform them what the other family members thought of them. Imagine the turmoil he created!

Some participants believe that this is too personal of an exercise, but when applying for an entry level job, they may be required to supply name, age, social security, address, number of children, ages. Right there, if you have a thirty-year-old woman, with a fifteen-year-old daughter, you have some information.

"So, my family looks like this," starts the group leader. "Notice that the schematic will be written on the board, but what will be spoken will be the narrative part of the genogram." The facilitator continues:

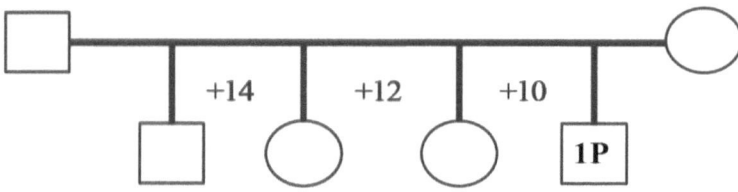

"What is interesting to note is, my brother is 14 years older than me, my older sister is 12 years older and my younger sister is 10 years old than me, so I am an only child with older siblings." The leader continues to expand upon the schematic and uses narrative to relate significant facts and anecdotes about the family members.

For instance, our birth order in the family can have a strong influence on who we are. Perhaps the youngest member of the family asks the same question after it has already been denied. The children want to go to the movies. The father says, "No, absolutely not, don't ask again, no movies, case closed!" Five minutes later, the youngest one in the family will approach the father, using a totally different tactic and ask, "When are we going to the movies?" And, the father, most likely will let the children go to the movies! All of these things add up to who we are.

What we also begin to notice are the trends within our families. There are health and addiction and behavioral patterns to examine.

When I learned I had high blood pressure, the first thing the doctor asked was, "Who else in your family suffers from high blood pressure?" I have to watch my weight, my diet, and exercise and take medication. These are also the issues for diabetes and other disorders. And, more importantly for genetic disorders like Tay-Sachs and sickle-cell anemia, which can indicate the need for genetic counseling.

Alcoholism and addiction are also seen to run through families and lead researchers to believe that there is a genetic flaw that causes one to be addictive. They don't know the exact answer. "But, what I do know, is, that if high blood pressure runs in my family, I need to take care of myself so I don't suffer from it. Likewise, if addiction runs in my family, I need to avoid addictive behavior, whether it is alcohol, drugs, prescription drugs, gambling, sex, food, whatever . . ." Thus, the leader concludes his genogram narrative.

Family systems therapist Bradshaw states that when a person views a genogram and sees addiction run rampant through generations, one often believes it is hopeless. But unlike the old cliché "one bad apple spoils the whole peck" one learns in recovery that one "good apple" can turn an entire family around. When that first family member has the guts to put down the bottle and make a stand for his or her life, then other members follow suit. It may not be one's closest relatives at first. More likely when the distant cousin hears that you got sober, they will be asking how you did it, and then momentum begins.

This is also true in incest. The victim feels so ashamed and is afraid to talk about what happened to anyone and believes it only happened to him or her. But, in reality if there is one victim in the family, more than likely there are others. The perpetrator did not stop with one child, but continued until caught. Once that first person is able to speak the truth about what happened, the other victims are more likely to come forward. The person has moved from being a victim to a survivor.

Instant therapy can also happen with genograms. The New York State Penal System allows small drug criminals to do their sentence in therapeutic communities, thinking that recovery programs are better than incarceration. One client, who was within a few months of completing his time at the therapeutic community, thought that speaking to a Family Therapist would hasten his release. He stated that he could go home and live with his Mother and that she would willingly sign whatever to get him home. His father, who lived in Puerto Rico, was to be returning to New York for some surgery and the client was definitely needed at home. The client was in his midthirties and was HIV positive. He started laying out his genogram:

His parents were married, although now geographically separated, had no children outside of their marriage, oldest daughter was in her fifties, in recovery; her son was twenty, incarcerated, an addict, HIV positive; the oldest brother was incarcerated, an addict, HIV positive; the second oldest the same; and so on for seven brothers, all incarcerated, addicts, and HIV positive. All through the session, the client stated what a good home he had grown up in and how loving his parents were. Upon completing the genogram, it was pointed out to him that if his parents were to have children who were all incarcerated, addicts, and HIV positive, would going home be a secure healthy environment for him?

The client became reflective and said he would think about it. As it turned out, he never broached the subject again, completed the program, found his own apartment and a great girlfriend, and was able to visit his mother, see his father at the hospital and not get caught up in whatever happened on the home front. Truly, that demonstrates the immediacy of a genogram.

Another client from Jamaica learned in completing her genogram that her father had siblings in Ethiopia. She immediately made plans to travel to Ethiopia to meet her unknown cousins.

Another client approached her therapist saying, "I don't know if I want to kill you or hug you! I have been up for over a week completing my genogram. I have learned so much about my family—some good, some not so good – but I now understand a lot more."

CHAPTER 15

The Keys to Success

I love to read biographies about great leaders throughout history.
What amazes me is the commonality of their experiences.
I don't recall any of them just starting out with great success.
There were risks. There were setbacks. There were losses. There were
failures. There were temptations. There were long periods of time
where nothing seemed to be going right.
—Rev. Terry A. Smith

When the famous psychiatrist Carl Jung, founder of analytic psychology, began practicing, he would have his patients talk about past traumas and memories. The hour for the therapeutic session would go by quickly and Jung realized that when the time was up he would send the person away still inundated with images of the past. Later Jung observed that having the person only talk about past history often sent the client away depressed, confused and struggling with these past memories. Some clients became despondent.

While people often resolved past issues, Jung realized the need to future orient his clients. Thus, toward the end of the therapy session he would ask, "What are you going to do?" (future tense) instead of asking "What happened?" (past tense). Jung found that getting the client "future oriented" lessened the chances of leaving depressed, and encouraged a more positive and enthusiastic outlook. He found that the future oriented person was more likely to be successful.

When author Tom Coleman was a freshman in college, he was doing poorly and was afraid of failing out of school. He was despondent and discouraged and couldn't understand why he couldn't grasp the academic material necessary to achieve good grades. While studying motivation in an Introduction to Psychology textbook, he discovered why. He learned the secrets of why some people were highly successful and some remained unsuccessful. By applying McClelland's *Keys to Success* personally, Dr. Coleman was able to move forward in his studies and career, and was then able to teach others how to achieve as well.

In the 1950s Harvard University professor Dr. David McClelland, inspired by a nineteenth-century sociologist Max Weber, undertook a massive study of past and contemporary human societies in an attempt to understand what made some civilizations great and others less so. McClelland presented his findings in a landmark book titled *The Achieving Society*. McClelland's research concluded that societies advanced the greatest when high achievement by members of society was facilitated by certain social policies and trends, and also when certain beliefs and behaviors were internalized by the individuals within their society.

Initially McClelland suspected that intelligence might be why people are successful in a myriad of aspects of society (e.g., school, business, economics, politics) but soon found that many highly gifted people don't necessarily go on to be very successful in society. Previously people taught that successful people are simply "smarter" than the rest but "Intelligence Tests" revealed that there are people with extremely high intelligence who are also homeless and unproductive. Instead McClelland found that people who are *highly motivated to achieve* are far more likely to succeed in fulfilling their dreams.

McClelland called this drive toward success *achievement motivation*, which he defined as the tendency to compete against standards of excellence. He defined "standards of excellence" as anything that motivates a person to work on and attempt to achieve some positive, morally and ethically higher accomplishment.

Examples of a High-Need Achiever's (Hi Nacher's) strivings could be:

1. A child attempting to build a sail boat that will sail across the lake.
2. A Thomas Edison who wants to invent a light bulb.
3. A teen who studies to win a spelling bee.
4. A person who wants to write a book.

McClelland found that when a person writes down one's fantasies, that the imaginings of a Hi Nacher would be filled with thoughts of attaining or wishing for "standards of excellence." The fantasies would be full of "goals of excellence." The more the person dreamed or wrote about these goals, the more likely one was to go out and find ways of achieving the goals. In other words the more a person wanted a particular goal, the more he or she was likely to translate that wish into action and make it happen.

The basic characteristics of persons that are high in Achievement Motivation include:

1. They Focus on the Future

High need achievers are hopeful and constantly looking to the future. They are always seeking opportunities and planning effective ways to achieve their goals. People that are lower in achievement motivation don't always recognize opportunity or goals when they present themselves. Focusing on the future can be a learned activity.

One client, Marvin, came to our group emaciated and weighing about 120 pounds. This middle aged man told the group about growing up poor in the "hood", that his mother had died and that his life had been a complete failure. We ran a pretend funeral for him where he talked to his mother and expressed his love, guilt and regrets to her. He cried copious tears for the first time in decades. As he continued to use his therapy groups, Marvin greatly improved in mental stability and in physical health. He was so motivated that he was hired to work with us and he started college. To his surprise he earned an A average in college and progressed quickly when he found that he had a tremendous potential. Marvin became a certified drug counselor, then director of a large substance abuse program, and then a college professor, while still helping us run sensitivity groups. From the once battered and down-beaten person, Marvin was able to succeed.

Depressed people tend to focus too much on the past, and addicted people focus only on the present. The farthest they can see into the future is their next "high." Like Marvin, healthy people tend to focus on the future. Healthy people get excited about the future and they are always planning more effective ways to achieve their next goal.

"'For I know the plans I have for you,' declares the Lord, 'plans to prosper you and not to harm you, plans to give you hope and a future'" (Jeremiah 29:11).

2. They Are Responsible

Harry Truman had a sign on his desk in the White House: "The buck stops here." He was taking responsibility for the outcome of his decisions and policies.

Psychiatrist William Glasser was given charge of the Ventura Drug Program for Girls in California. In this program for young women he found that every one of his charges was highly skilled in manipulation. At first he tried medications on the clients, but found that did little to help the members become "drug free." He realized that if they were going to become "drug free," he would have to teach them to become responsible. If their behavior in the school was less than responsible, he would give them a "learning experience." In other words, there would be a consequence if they failed to be responsible.

Generally Glasser believed that a mentally healthy person is a responsible person and a mentally ill (unsuccessful person) is irresponsible. He believed that it is vital that society teach responsibility for a society to succeed. Glasser said, "Responsibility, a concept basic to Reality Therapy, is defined as the ability to fulfill one's needs, and to do so in a way that does not deprive others of the ability to fulfill their needs . . . A responsible person also does that which gives him a feeling of self worth and a feeling that he is worthwhile to others. He is motivated to strive and perhaps endure privation to attain self-worth . . . People do not act irresponsibly because they are ill; they are ill because they act irresponsibly" (p 13).

"For we must all appear before the judgment seat of Christ, so that each of us may receive what is due us for the things done while in the body, whether good or bad" (2 Cor. 5:10).

3. They Work far Achievement, Not Money

"You can't live a perfect day without doing something for someone who will never be able to repay you" (John Wooden).

Think of many of the achievements of your life, such as graduating, presenting a paper, winning a game, having a role in a play. Did you do it for money or was it for the joy of achieving?

Psychologists did a research study in which they gave a happiness questionnaire to a group of people in the morning. They then gave each person twenty dollars and said to half of them to spend it on themselves by the end of the day. They told the other half to spend the twenty dollars on someone else by the end of the day. They gave the same happiness questionnaire to all of them at the end of the day. The ones who gave the money away scored higher in happiness.

The famous German doctor, Albert Schweitzer, gave up a lucrative medical practice to move to Africa and dedicate his life to healing sick people. Dr. Schweitzer spent his life unselfishly helping others; not only was he an extremely high in achievement motivation but also he was very happy.

"So do not worry, saying 'What shall we eat?' or 'What shall we drink?' or 'What shall we wear?' For the pagans run after all these things, and your heavenly father knows that you need them. But seek first his kingdom and his righteousness, and all these things will be given to you as well" (Matthew 6:31–33).

4. They Are Highly Competitive

"Success is peace of mind which is a direct result of self-satisfaction in knowing you did your best to become the best that you are capable of becoming" (John Wooden).

In sports each competitor is taught less to focus on beating the opponent and more on doing their best. A high need achiever is taught to compete against herself. The idea is to not make others less, but to present your best performance. The goal of a high need achiever on a team is to help the whole team turn out the best performance possible, rather than to be the showboat who tries to get all of the glory and put most of the points on the score board.

As an individual, in the workplace or in the arena, one is always urged to "be the best you can be!" With long hours of effective study or practice, personal, as well as professional, goals may be achieved.

"Do you not know that in a race all the runners run, but only one gets the prize. Run in such a way as to get the prize" (1 Cor. 9:24).

5. They Take Moderate Risks

McClelland found that people who are low in achievement motivation may:

a. Be more prone to gamble. Gambling is risky behavior, has impoverished multitudes, and can become a serious addiction for some.

b. Be lazier than others. These people may take no risks at all.

c. Be more unassertive or be over assertive and aggressive. Religions that teach meditation and passivity and religions that teach aggression and hostility tend to produce persons who are lower in achievement motivation. When aggression arises out of hostility, and may lead to violence and destruction, it is the antithesis of achieving.

d. Quit very easily, and are more fearful than others. They become overwhelmed by fear of success or fear of failure and they aren't as likely to follow through.

When "free stuff" is offered to the public, low need achievers are far more likely to flock to get the freebies. High achievers are more likely to know that when something is advertised as free, there is often some catch and that few things in life are truly free. Likewise, high need achievers generally do not inhabit gambling casinos as they know the odds are stacked against a long term win. Conversely, people that are high in the need to achieve take moderate risks rather than no risk or actions that are too risky.

People believe there are a myriad of obstacles that can prevent them from being successful but often the biggest obstacle is one's own false belief, or fear of failure. "God is not the author of Fear." People who are low in achievement are often full of fears. There are basically two types of fear that haunt low need achievers. First is *fear of failure*. When this fear is so intense, the low achiever won't even try.

The second fear is *fear of success*. The negative self talk goes something like this: "If I take that promotion, the job will be too much for me, and I will fail."

Psychologists teach that *fear* equals *false evidence appearing real*.

Teaching *healthy self-talk* (the ability to say positive affirming things to one's self and then to act upon them) becomes essential for achievement.

Using "I can" phrases is more likely to help people believe in themselves and to help achieve their goals.

6. They Believe They Can Achieve

Psychologist Albert Bandura (1997) found that highly successful people possess a very important characteristic which he called self-efficacy. Bandura learned that people with high self-efficacy believe they can perform well and are more likely to view difficult tasks as something to be mastered rather than something to be avoided. When Marvin started to heal emotionally and physically, not only did he start to focus on the future, but also he began to believe that he had God-given potentials. He started to "believe he could be highly successful." Marvin, through getting regular therapy, coping with his hurts, and developing healthy goals, grew into self-efficacy. Marvin learned healthy self-talk. Not only did Marvin develop extremely high self-efficacy, but in his work as a counselor and group leader Marvin also helped instill those same positive attitudes in others. His testimony inspired many. He was instrumental in helping hundreds of people not only become drug-free, but also motivated them to live to their highest potential.

7. They Are Highly Resilient

"Do not judge me by my success. Judge me by how many times I fell down and got back up" (Nelson Mandela).

Resilience means "we fall down but we get up." People who refuse to stay down are far more likely to succeed. A resilient person does more positive self talk and refuses to wallow in the past. To imitate this behavior and way of thinking enables one to be far more likely to succeed.

"For though the righteous fall seven times, they rise again. But the wicked stumble when calamity strikes" (Proverbs 24:16).

8. They Accept Mentoring

"A coach is someone who can give correction without causing resentment" (John Wooden).

It is essential to be open minded and receptive to mentoring. Remember a time you were mentored. How do you feel about the experience? Was there any resistance on your part to the mentoring? What did you do as a result? What were some of the barriers for your accepting help? How did you thank your mentor?

People who are high in achievement motivation know they don't have all of the answers and are constantly reaching out for more information on how to proceed into a successful life. For instance a person who wants to invest in the stock market must learn about the stock market and eventually know some of the following: What is the Dow or the S and P 500? How are stocks different from bonds? What are mutual funds and what is an IRA? People who want to be competent seek ways to educate themselves as much as possible about the topic at hand. Conversely, psychologists have found out that people who have a tendency to believe that they are "right," often do not seek advice.

Paul, as a follower of Jesus, said in Titus, "You must teach what is in accord with sound doctrine. Teach the older men to be temperate, worthy of respect, self-controlled, and sound in faith, in love and in endurance" (Titus 2: 1).

9. They Are Morally and Spiritually Grounded

"Successful people pray" (John Wooden).

High need achievers tend to be moral and ethical. Rodney Stark, in his book *The Victory of Reason: How Christianity Led to Freedom, Capitalism, and Western Success*, states, "The rise of the West, including the rise of science, rested entirely on religious foundations, and the people who brought it about were devout Christians." He explains that in a highly achieving society, morality, and spirituality (namely, Christianity) were and are vital to making high achievers, who in turn improve the economic level of society.

Stark says, "At the start of the twentieth century, the German sociologist Max Weber published what soon became an immensely influential study: *The Protestant Ethic and the Spirit of Capitalism.* In it he proposed that capitalism originated only in Europe because, of all the world's religions, only Protestantism provided a moral vision that led people to restrain their material consumption while vigorously seeking wealth. Weber argued that prior to the Reformation, restraint on consumption was invariably linked to asceticism and hence to condemnations of commerce. Conversely, the pursuit of wealth was linked to profligate consumption. Either cultural pattern was inimical to capitalism. According to Weber, the Protestant ethic shattered these traditional linkages, creating a culture of frugal entrepreneurs content to systematically reinvest profits in order to pursue ever greater wealth, and therein lies the key to capitalism and the ascendancy of the West" (p. xi).

Some studies suggest that the average worker in the world makes less than ten dollars a day, but the average American over the last two hundred years has made more than twice the per capita income than that of the next most successful country in the world, namely England. Stark, Weber and McClelland all agree that the principles of Christianity which teach the work ethic, frugality, morality, responsibility, and cooperation are integral in becoming successful (not only monetarily but also in terms of any higher achievement.)

Movie director and play writer Tyler Perry said, "If you are successful it is thereby the Grace of God." He continued by saying, "Pick one goal and plant one seed and water it daily. Keep working at it and it will eventually grow and bear fruit. In the 1990's I borrowed $12,000 and set up a play but only 30 people came and I knew all of them. Year after year I worked and believed and God finally came through."

"The house of the righteous contains great treasure, but the income of the wicked brings ruin" (Proverbs 15: 6).

10. They Are Always Successful If They Remain High in Achievement Motivation and Refuse to Quit

"Goals are dreams with deadlines" (Hal Urban).

When David McClelland measured the level of achievement motivation in America in recent times compared to previous times and he found that over a hundred years ago Achievement Motivation was higher than now. It reigned over other motives that seem more common today (e.g., the need for power, affiliation, sex and violence).

One of the reasons that it was far higher in the 1900s was the great amount of immigrants drawn here for a "better life." They viewed the United States as the land of opportunity and they brought a new vitality to the United States that raised the capitalist spirit and the "work ethic" to new levels. This work ethic was validated by Henry Ford who raised his workers' salaries so they could afford to buy the Model T Fords that they were manufacturing in Ford's innovative assembly line. Also Thomas Edison was demonstrating the limitless possibilities that could be achieved in his inventions of electricity, light bulb, phonograph and motion pictures.

At that time the most common theme seen in the literature was achievement motivation; people saw the United States as a place of limitless opportunity. In the early 1900s some of the bestselling books were written by Horatio Alger. His books all had the same *from-rags-to-riches* theme. The books were about a young person who started out poor (a shoe shine boy) and through hard work and reinvestment became rich (owner of a shoe factory). Horatio Alger in his novel, *Do and Dare,* concludes:

> Herbert and his mother have moved to Boston. Our hero is learning business in the counting-room of Mr. Compton. They live in a pleasant house at the South End, and Mr. Melville is now restored to a very fair measure of health, is boarding, or, rather, has his home with them. He is devoting his time to literary pursuits, and I am told that he is the author of a brilliant paper in a recent number of the *North American Review.* Herbert finds some time for study, and under the guidance of his friend and former employer, he has already become a very creditable scholar in French, German, and English literature. He enjoys his present prosperity all the better for the hardships through which he passed before reaching it.

In some populations achievement motivation has declined in America (*Achieving Society* chapter 3) which McClelland said will eventually lead to an economic down turn. However, McClelland also stated that even if the level of motivation is low in others, the person who is motivated can still be very successful because he will see the opportunities for advancement and achieving that others don't see. Often people who come from foreign countries are the highest in achievement motivation, no matter their religion, because they see the tremendous opportunities in the US and find ways to take advantage of these opportunities. Studies indicate that when immigrants are given the projective personality test, called the Thematic Apperception Test, they score much higher in Achievement Motivation than the average American.

When working at a community college we wondered why the graduation rate was so low. After measuring the level of Achievement Motivation of the community college population, we learned two year students had much lower levels of motivation than four year college students, which helped to explain the higher dropout rate and lower graduation rate. McClelland was invited to send representatives to our school to see if they could teach achievement motivation to our students. McClelland sent Herb.

Herb told his story. He grew up in a tough part of Boston (Roxbury) and as an adolescent became drug addicted and did not finish high school. He explained that he would do anything to get his heroin and alienated all of his family members and often got in trouble with the law. One day he heard that McClelland was "coming to the hood" to teach his people how to succeed. Herb said he went to the meeting to give this Harvard Professor a hard time, because he believed that this rich professor could never fathom the prejudice and poverty "his people" had suffered. He said he sat in the front of the room and argued earnestly with the professor. After the presentation, they broke up into groups and each group member was asked to share their future goals.

When it came to Herb's turn to share he said, "I want to open a restaurant." The group members asked him *how* he was going to achieve that goal. Herb was dumbfounded. He had alienated all of his family and all of his money was going to drugs. The group leader said, "Come next week and share with us your plan on opening a restaurant."

Herb got convicted and actually started to plan how to make this dream come true. He went to a cousin, who owned a small grocery store and told him he would volunteer his time and clean his store and stack shelves if his cousin would feed him and give him a place to sleep. His cousin reluctantly conceded but said if he found he was "high on drugs" he would have to go. Herb said he stopped getting high and worked very hard. At the meeting the next week he told the group he was going to save money and open up a small hamburger stand.

With each Need Achievement group meeting Herb grew more confident and learned what it would take to achieve his goal. Five years had passed from that first meeting and Herb had since bought two abandoned buildings in different parts of town, fixed them up and opened up restaurants. He said he had also just graduated from a community college with honors and had five hundred saved in the bank.

How to Run Groups That Increase Achievement Motivation

1.   Measure motivation

Have each group member measure his or her level of achievement motivation. To do this, McClelland used the Thematic Apperception Test (TAT), introduced by Henry Murray. He showed the group members a picture of a person hanging onto a rope and had them tell a story about that person. He had them tell the story by using their fantasies and answering three questions:

a.   How did this person get here? (talks about the past)

b.   What is the person doing now? (present)

c.   What will happen? (future)

Using these questions teach the participants to score their fantasy stories for Achievement Motivation. To have individual group members write and score their own responses for achievement is in itself quite motivating.

One point is given for Achievement Motivation when the person in the imagined story writes that the person is striving to achieve some "standard of excellence" (e.g., climb to the top of a mountain or pass the rope climbing test to get into the Navy Seal Corps). Generally if the person has at least three standards of excellence images in a one page story, they tend to be high in achievement motivation. Lower than the three standards of excellence ranks them as needing some motivation training. These are the candidates who usually benefit from the achievement groups.

2.   Teach self-efficacy

A person who is high in self efficacy is one who believes he can achieve whatever he sets out to do. Because almost everyone has intense inferiority feelings and self doubts, group members are taught "healthy self talk." The group is not allowed to tolerate any failure talk. Participants are taught to think and act at all times in terms of standards of excellence. The group members are encouraged to help each other in getting rid of "stinking thinking" and replace it with "healthy self talk." In this way the members start to truly believe they can do what they fantasize. They will then be willing to sacrifice and to work hard at achieving their goals.

3.   Review keys to success and support one another

Teach clients to focus on imitating and believing in the ten principles discussed above. These characteristics are reinforced at the beginning of each group before each member talks about his or her week's progress. The group should challenge one another to standards of excellence and help to build up each other's self confidence. Group members are to offer support and encouragement and helpful suggestions to help each other achieve their goals.

4.   Establish specific goals and objectives

Supply clients with a premade sheet to fill in individual goals, especially vocational ones. Include specific objectives and a time line for specific activities.

1.   List your goals for the future . . .
2.   What are you going to do today to work toward these goals?
3.   What are you going to do this week, this month, this year?
4.   Where will you be in one year, five years?

Then gather the group at least once a week to talk about these goals and have members tell the others how they are progressing toward their goals. Encourage the person to do something every day toward reaching his or her dreams. Also challenge the person to develop a step by step approach, with specific activities, to achieving one's goals. Define what each is doing to educate or what steps are being taken to further the goals. Some group members may readjust their goals and may even replace them with updated goals. This is permissible, as long as they are working toward the future, and believing that they can achieve. Healthy group pressure, encouragement, and accountability are powerful in stimulating the person on to success.

CHAPTER 16

The Journey Is Yours

We live by choice, not by chance.

—Hal Urban

Begin now.

BIBLIOGRAPHY

Abramson, L. Y., Seligman, M. E. P., & Teasdale, J. (1978). Learned helplessness in humans: Critique and reformulation. *Journal of Abnormal Psychology*, 87, 49-74.

Adler, A. (1959). *Understanding human nature*. New York: Premier Books.

Agosti, V. (1995). The efficiency of treatments in reducing alcohol consumption: A meta-analysis. *International Journal of the Addictions*, 30, 1067-1077.

Alger, Horatio. (1884). *Do or Dare*. New York: Porter & Coates.

American Psychological Association. (1967). *Casebook on ethical standards of psychologists*. Washington, DC: Author.

Antonuccio, D., Thomas, M. & Danton, W. G. (1997). A cost-effectiveness analysis of cognitive behavior therapy and fluoxetine (prozac) in the treatment of depression. *Behavior Therapy*, 28, 187-210.

Aponte, H.J., & Van Deusen, J.M. Structural Family Therapy. In A.S. Gurman and D.P. Kniskern (Eds.). (1981). *Handbook of Family Therapy*. New York: Brunner/Mazel, 1981.

Bach, G. R. (1954). *Intensive Group Psychotherapy*. New York: Ronald Press.

Bandura, A. (1969). *Principles of behavior modification*. New York: Holt, Rinehart, & Winston.

Bandura, A. (1986). *Social foundations of thought and action: A social cognitive theory*. Englewood Cliffs, NJ: Prentice-Hall.

Bandura, A. (1997). *Self –efficacy: The exercise of control.* New York: W. H. Freemen.

Bandura, A. (Ed.). (1971). *Psychological Modeling.* Chicago: Aldine-Atherton.

Barnes, G. (Ed.). (1977). *Transactional Analysis After Eric Berne.* New York: Harper College Press.

Beck, A. T. (1967). *Depression: Clinical, experimental, and theoretical aspects.* New York: Harper & Row.

Beck, A. T. (1976). *Cognitive therapy and the emotional disorders.* New York: International Universities Press.

Beck, A. T., Rush, A. J., Shaw, B. F., & Emery, G. (1979). *Cognitive therapy of depression: A treatment manual.* New York: Guilford Press.

Beck, A., Rush, A., Shaw, B., and Emery, G. (1979). *Cognitive Therapy Of Depression.* New York: Guilford Press.

Beck, A.T. *Depression. Causes And Treatment.* (1975). Philadelphia: University of Pennsylvania Press.

Beck, A.T. (1976). *Cognitive Therapy And Emotional Disorders.* New York: International Universities Press.

Bellack, A. S., & Hersen, M. (Eds.). (1998). *Behavioral assessment: A practical handbook* (4th ed.). Boston: Allyn & Bacon.

Bellack, A. S., & Mueser, K. T. (1994). Schizophrenia. In L. W. Craighead, W. E. Craighead, A. E. Kazdin, & M. J. Mahoney (Eds.), *Cognitive and behavioral interventions: An empirical approach to mental health problems* (pp. 105-122). Boston: Allyn & Bacon.

Berne, E. *Games People Play.* (1964). New York: Grove Press.

Berne, E. *Transactional Analysis In Psychotherapy.* (1961). New York: Grove Press.

Bible, New International Version. (1985). Grand Rapids, Michigan: Zondervan Bible Publishers.

Bohart, A. C., & Tallman, K. (1998). The person as active agent in experiential therapy. In L.S. Greenberg & J. C. Watson (Eds.), *Handbook of experiential psychotherapy* (pp. 178-200). New York: Guilford Press.

Botvin, G. J. (1999). Adolescent drug abuse prevention: Current finding and future directions. In M. D. Glantz, D. Meyer, & C. R. Hartel (Eds.), *Drug abuse: Origins and interventions* (pp. 285-308). Washington, DC: American Psychological Association.

Bouton, M. E., & Swartzentruber, D. (1991). Sources of relapse after extinction in Pavlovian and instrumental learning. *Clinical Psychology Review*: 11, 123-140.

Bowen, M. (1976). Theory in the Practice of Psychology. In P. Guerin (Ed.) Family *Therapy.* New York: Gardner Press.

Bradshaw, J. (1995). *Family Secrets.* New York: Bantam Books.

Brammer, Lawrence. (1979). *The Helping Relationship: Process And Skills.* Englewood Cliffs, NJ: Prentice-Hall, Inc.

Burke, J. (1989). *Contemporary Approaches to Psychotherapy and Counseling.* Belmont, CA: Brooks/Cole Publishing.

Burns, D. (1981). *Feeling Good. The New Mood Therapy.* New York: New American Library.

Carnegie, Dale. (1936). *How To Win Friends And Influence People.* New York: Pocket Books.

Carson, R. (1988). *Abnormal Psychology and Modern Life*. Glenview, Illinois: Scott, Foresman.

Casriel, D. (1972). *A Scream Away From Happiness*. New York: Grosset & Dunlap.

Clay, Rebecca. (2013). *Minding the Heart*. APA Monitor.

Colbert, Don, MD. (2003) *Deadly Emotions*. Nashville: Thomas Nelson Publishers.

Coleman, Thomas R., and Cunningham, Roger. (2004). *Psychotherapy As a Contact Sport*. New York: Whittier Publications, Inc.

Collins, G. (1988). *Can You Trust Psychology?* Downers Grove, Illinois: InterVarsity Press.

Corey, G. (1985). *Theory and Practice of Group Counseling*. Monterey, CA: Brooks/Cole.

Corey, G., Corey, M., and Callanan, P. (1979). *Professional And Ethical Issues In Counseling And Psychotherapy*. Monterey, CA: Brooks/Cole.

Cory, G. (1999). *Theory And Practice Of Counseling And Psychotherapy*. Brooks/Cole Publishing Co.: Monterey, CA.

Dossey, L. (1996). *Prayer is Good Medicine*. San Francisco: Harper Collins Publishers, Inc.

Drakeford, J. (1961). *Counseling For Church Leaders*. Nashville, Tenn: Broadman Press.

Duvall, E. (1977). *Marriage and Family Development*. (5th ed.). New York: J.B. Lippincott.

Ellis, A. (1994). *Reason and emotion in psychotherapy, revised and updated*. New York: Carol Publishing.

Ellis, A. (2000). Rational-emotive behavior therapy as an internal control psychology. *Journal of Rational-Emotive and Cognitive Behavior Therapy*, 18, 19-38.

Ellis, A. (1973). *Humanistic Psychotherapy: The Rational Emotive Approach*. New York: Julian Press.

Ellis, A. (1984). *Rational Emotive Therapy And Pastoral Counseling: A Reply To Richard Wessler*. Personnel and Guidance Journal, 62.

Ellis, A. *The Essence Of RET-1984*. Journal of Rational Emotive Therapy, 2(1), 19-25.

Ellis, A., & Grieger, R. (Eds.). (1977). *Handbook of rational-emotive therapy*. New York: Springer.

Evans, Jimmy. (2013). *The Hurt Pocket, Breaking the Legacy of Pain*. Marriage Today

Evans, R. (1975). *Carl Rogers: The Man And His Ideas*. New York: Dutton.

Fagan, J., and Shepherd, I. (Eds.). (1970). *What Is Gestalt Therapy?* New York: Harper and Row.

Fretz, B., and Mills, D. (1980). *Licensing And Certification Of Psychologists And Counselors*. San Francisco: Jossey-Bass.

Gazda, G. M. (1984). *Group Counseling: A Developmental Approach* (2nd ed.). Boston: Allyn & Bacon.

Glasser, William, MD. (1965). *Reality Therapy*. New York: Harper and Row.

Gladding, S. (1988). *Counseling*. Columbus, OH: Merrill Publisher.

Goldenberg, I. & Goldenberg, H. (1985). *Family Therapy: An Overview Second Edition*. Monterey, CA: Brooks/Cole Publishing.

Goleman, D. (1995). *Emotional intelligence*. New York: Bantam Books.

Goulding, M., and Goulding, R. (1979). *Changing Lives Through Redecision Therapy*. New York: Brunner/Mazel.

Guerin, P. & Pendagast, E. (1976). Evaluation of family system and genogram. In P. Guerin (ed.). *Family therapy*. New York: Gardner Press.

Hall, C. S. & Nordby, V. J. (1973). *A Primer of Jungian Psychology*. New York: New American Library.

Harris, T. (1967). *I'm Ok – You're Ok*. New York: Avon.

Hergenhahn, B. R. (1998). *An Introduction to the History of Psychology*. Pacific Grove, CA: Brooks/Cole Publishing Company.

Hobbs, N. Group Centered Psychotherapy. In C. R. Rogers (ed.). (1951). *Client Centered Therapy*. Boston: Houghton Mifflin, 1951.

Hoffman, L. (1981). *Foundations of Family Therapy*. New York: Basic Books.

Howland, R.H., & Thase, M.E. (1999). Affective disorders: Biological aspects. In T. Millon, P.H. Blaney, & R.D. Davis (Eds.), *Oxford textbook of psychopathology* (pp. 166-202). New York: Oxford University Press.

Ivey, A.E. (1995). Psychotherapy as liberation: Toward specific skills and strategies in multicultural counseling and therapy. In J.G. Ponterotto & J.M. Casas (Eds.), *Handbook of multicultural counseling* (pp. 53-72). Thousand Oaks, CA: Sage.

Ivey, A.E., Ivey, M.B., & Simek-Downing, L. (1987). *Counseling and psychotherapy: Integrating skills, theory, and practice*. Englewood Cliffs, NJ: Prentice-Hall.

Jung, C. G. (1933). *Modern man in search of a soul*. New York: Harcourt, Brace.

Jung, C. G. (1935/1956). *Collected works: Two essays on analytical psychology*. (Vol. 17). Princeton, NJ: Princeton University Press.

Kanfer, F. H., & Goldstein, A. P. (Eds.). (1991). *Helping people change: A textbook of methods* (4th ed.). New York: Pergamon Press.

Kidd, Susan Monk. (2002). *The Secret Life of Bees.* New York: Viking.

Kirwan, W. (1984). *Biblical Concepts In Christian Counseling.* Grand Rapids, MI: Baker Book House.

Kohut, H. (1971). *The analysis of the self.* New York: International Universities Press.

Kohut, H. (1977). *The restoration of the self.* New York: International Universities Press.

Korchin, S. (1976). *Modern clinical psychology: Principles of intervention in the clinic and community.* New York: Basic Books.

Latner, J. (1973). *Gestalt Therapy Book.* New York: Bantam Books.

Lazarus, R. S. (1991). *Emotion and adaptation.* New York: Oxford University Press.

Lazarus, R. S. (1991). *Stress and emotion: A new synthesis.* New York: Springer.

Lewinsohn, P. M. (1974). A behavioral approach to depression. In R.J. Friedman & M. M. Katz (Eds.), *The psychology of depression: Contemporary theory and research* (pp. 157-185). New York: John Wiley.

Lewinsohn, P. M., & Gotlib, I. H. (1995). Behavioral theory and treatment of depression. In E. E. Beckham & W. R. Leber (Eds.), *Handbook of depression* (2nd ed., pp. 352-375). New York: Guilford Press.

Lewinsohn, P. M., Allen, N. B., Seeley, J. R., & Gotlib, I. H. (1999). First onset versus recurrence of depression: Differential processes of psychosocial risk. *Journal of Abnormal Psychology*, 108, 483-489.

Lichtenstein, E. (1980). *Psychotherapy: Approaches And Applications.* Monterey, CA: Brooks/Cole Publishing Co.

LoPiccolo, J. (1978). "Direct treatment of sexual dysfunction." J. LoPiccolo and L. LoPiccolo (Eds.). *Handbook Of Sex Therapy*. New York: Plenum Press.

LoPiccolo, J. and LoPiccolo L. (1978). (Eds.). *Handbook Of Sex Therapy*. New York: Plenum Press.

Lorenz, K. (1966). *On aggression*. New York: Harcourt, Brace & World.

Magden, S., & Shostrom, E. (1974). Unpublished paper presented to annual meeting of American Psychological Association, New Orleans.

Mahoney, M. (1998). Essential themes in the training of psychotherapists. *Psychotherapy in Private Practice*, 17, 43-59.

Mahoney, M. J. (1974). *Cognition and behavior modification*. Cambridge, MA: Ballinger.

Maletsky, B. (1980). *Self-Centered Versus Court-Referred Sexually Deviant Patients; Behavior Therapy*, 11, 306-314.

Marino, J. L. (1959). *Psychodrama*. New York: Beacon House.

Maslow, A. (1996). *The psychology of science: A reconnaissance*. New York: Harper & Row.

Maslow, A. H. (1971*). The farther reaches of human nature*. New York: Viking.

Maslow, A. H. (1987). *Motivation and personality*. (3rd ed.). New York: Harper & Row.

Masters, W.H., and Johnson, V. E. (1970). *Human Sexual Response*. Boston: Little, Brown.

May, R., & Yalom, I.D. (1989). Existential psychotherapy. In R.J. Corsini & D. Wedding (Eds.). *Current psychotherapies* (4th ed., pp. 363-402). Itasca, IL: F. E. Peacock.

McClelland, D. C. & Jemmott, J.B. (1980). Power motivation, stress, and physical illness. *Journal of Human Stress*, 6, 6-15.

McClelland, D. C. (1961). *The achieving society.* Princeton, NJ: Van Nostrand.

McClelland, D. C. (1985). How motives, skills, and values determine what people do. *American Psychologist*, 40, 812-825.

McClelland, D. C., Alexander, C., & Marks, E. (1982). The need for power, stress, immune function, and illness among male prisoners. *Journal of Abnormal Psychology*, 91, 61-70.

McClelland, D. C., Atkinson, J. W., Clark, R. A., & Lowell, E. L. (1976). *The achievement motive.* New York: Irvington.

McClelland, D.C. (1965). Achievement and entrepreneurship. *Journal of Personality and Social Psychology*, 10, 389-392.

McGoldrick, M. & Gerson, R. (1985). *Genograms in family assessment.* New York: W. W. Norton.

McGoldrick, M. (1995). *You can go home again.* New York: W.W. Norton & Company.

Meichenbaum, D. (1977). *Cognitive-behavior modification: An integrative approach.* New York: Plenum.

Meichenbaum, D. (1995). Cognitive-behavioral therapy in historical perspective. In B. Bongar & L.E. Beutler (eds.), *Comprehensive textbook of psychotherapy: Theory and practice* (pp. 140-158). New York: Oxford University Press.

Minuchin, S. & Fishman, H.C. (1981). *Family Therapy Techniques.* Cambridge, MA: Harvard University Press.

Minuchin, (1974). S. *Families and Family Therapy.* Cambridge, MA: Harvard University Press.

Moreno, J.L. (1946). *Psychodrama* (Vol. 1, 2ⁿᵈ ed.). New York: Beacon House.

Moreno, J.L. Psychodrama. In S. Arieti (Ed.). (1959). American *Handbook of Psychiatry* (Vol. 2). New York: Basic Books.

Murray, H. A. (1938). *Explorations in Personality*. New York: Oxford University Press.

Papp, P. (1973). Family sculpting in preventive work with "well" families. *Family Process*. 12, 197-212.

Passons, W.R. (1975). *Gestalt Approaches In Counseling*. New York: Holt Rinehart and Winston.

Patterson, C.H. (2000) Understanding *Psychotherapy*. Ross-on-Wye, England: PCCS Books.

Peris, F. (1969). *Gestalt Therapy Verbatim*. Moab, Utah: Real People Press.

Peris, F. (1969). *In And Out Of The Garbage Pail*. Moab, Utah: Real People Press.

Peris, F. (1973). *The Gestalt Approach And Eye Witness To Therapy*. New York: Bantam Books.

Pietrofesa, J., Hoffman, A., & Splete, H. (1984). *Counseling: An Introduction* (2ⁿᵈ ed.). Boston: Houghton Mifflin.

Polster, E. and Polster, M. (1973). *Gestalt Therapy Integrated*. New York: Brunner/Mazel.

Rank, O. (1936). *Truth and reality. A life history of the human will*. NY: Knopf.

Rank, O. (1936). *Will therapy; and, Truth and reality*. NY: Knopf.

Ritter, K.Y. (1982). Training Group Counselors: A total curriculum perspective. *Journal for Specialists in Group Work*. 7, 226-274.

Rogers, C. & Wood, J. (1974). "Client-centered theory: Carl Rogers. "In A. Burton (ED.), *Operational Theories Of Personality*. New York: Brunner/Mazel.

Rogers, C. (1957). "The necessary and sufficient condition of therapeutic personality change." *Journal Of Consulting Psychology*.

Rogers, C. (1980). *A Way Of Being*. Palo Alto, CA: Houghton Mifflin.

Rogers, C. (1951). *Counseling And Psychotherapy*. Boston: Houghton Mifflin.

Rogers, C. (1961). *On Becoming A Person*. Boston: Houghton Mifflin.

Rogers, C. R. (1949a). The attitude and orientation of the counselor in client-centered therapy. *Journal of Consulting Psychology*, 13, 82-94.

Rogers, C. R. (1951). *Client-centered therapy: Its current practice, implications, and theory*. Boston: Houghton Mifflin.

Rogers, C. R. (1952). "Client-entered" psychotherapy. *Scientific American*, 187, 66-74.

Rogers, C. R. (1954). *Psychotherapy and personality change*. Chicago: University of Chicago Press.

Rogers, C.R. Kirshcenbaum, H., & Henderson, V. L. (Eds.). (1989). The Carl Rogers Reader. Boston, M.A. Houghton Mifflin.

Rotter, J. B. (1954). *Social learning and clinical psychology*. New York: Prentice-Hall.

Sarason, I. G. & Sarason, B.R. (1999). *Abnormal Psychology*. New Jersey. Prentice-Hall.

Satir, V.M. (1967). Cojoint Family Therapy. Palo Alto, CA: Science & Behavior Books.

Schmidt, Stuart. (1987). "The Perils of Persistence." *Psychology Today*. November, p.32.

Seligman, M. E. P. (1975). Helplessness: *On depression, development, and death.* San Francisco: W.H. Freeman.

Seligman, M. E. P. (1994). *What you can change and what you can't: The complete guide to successful self-improvement.* New York: Knopf.

Skinner, B.F. (1971). *Beyond Freedom And Dignity.* New York: Knopf.

Slavson, S.R. (1947). *The Practice of Group Psychotherapy.* New York: International University Press.

Smith, M.L., Glass, G.V., & Miller, T.I. (1980). *The benefits of psychotherapy.* Baltimore: Johns Hopkins University Press.

Smith, Terry. (2011). *TEN: How would you rate your Life?* Oviedo, Florida: Higher Life Development Services, Inc.

Spiegler, M.D. (1998). *Contemporary behavior therapy* (3rd ed.). Pacific Grove, CA: Brooks/Cole.

Stampfl, T. (1973). *Implosive Therapy: Theory And Technique.* Morristown, N.J. General Learning Press.

Stampfl, T. (1975). "Implosive Therapy." *Psychology Today*, February.

Stark, R. (2005). The Victory of Reason. New York: Random House.

Stuart, R.B. (1980). *Helping Couples Change.* New York: Guilford Press.

Sundberg, N. (1981). *Introduction to Clinical Psychology.* Englewood Cliffs, NJ: Prentice Hall Inc.

Sundbert, Norman et. al. (1983). Introduction *To Clinical Psychology.* NJ: Prentice-Hall, Inc.

Swihart, J. & Richardson, G. (1987). *Counseling In Times Of Crisis.* Waco, Texas: Word Books.

Van Hoose, W., and Kottler, J. (1977). *Ethical And Legal Issues In Counseling And Psychotherapy.* San Francisco: Jossey-Bass.

White, J & Blue, K. (1985). *Healing The Wounded.* Downers Grove, Illinois: InterVarsity Press.

Wolfe, B.E. & Sigl, P. (1998). Experiential psychotherapy of the anxiety disorders. In L.S. Greenberg & J.C. Watson (Eds.), *Handbook of experiential psychotherapy* (pp. 272-294). New York: Guilford Press.

Wolpe, J. and Lazarus, (1975). A. *Behavior Therapy Techniques.* New York: Wiley.

Wolpe, J. (1969). *The Practice Of Behavior Therapy.* New York: Pergamon Press.

Woody, S.R., & Sanderson, W.C. (1998). Manuals for empirically supported treatments: 1998 update. *The Clinical Psychologist,* 51, 17-21.

Wynne, L.C. (1958). Pseudomutuality in the family relations of schizophrenics. *Psychiatry,* 21, 205-220.

Yalom, I. D. (1975). *The Theory and Practice of Group Psychotherapy.* (2nd ed.). New York: Basic Books.

Yalom, I., Lieberman, M., & Miles, M. A. (1971). Study of Encounter Group Casualties. *Archives of General Psychiatry.* 25, 16-30.

Yalom, Y.D. (1980). *The theory and practice of group psychotherapy* (4th ed.). New York: Basic Books.

Young, A.S., Klap, R., Sherbourne, C.D., & Wells, K.B. (2001). The quality of care for depressive and anxiety disorders in the United States. *Archives of General Psychiatry,* 58, 55-61.